Property of

_____

Table of Contents

Cover Background Image by Lori A. Melroy

Regions of the US

Northeast

Southeast

Midwest

Rockies

Southwest

Pacific NW

West

3

States by Region

Northeast
- Connecticut
- Delaware
- District of Columbia
- Maine
- Maryland
- Massachusetts
- New Hampshire
- New Jersey
- New York
- Pennsylvania
- Rhode Island
- Vermont

Southeast
- Alabama
- Florida
- Georgia
- Kentucky
- Louisiana
- Mississippi
- North Carolina
- Puerto Rico
- South Carolina
- Tennessee
- Virgin Islands
- Virginia
- West Virginia

Midwest
- Arkansas
- Illinois
- Indiana
- Iowa
- Kansas
- Michigan
- Minnesota
- Missouri
- Nebraska
- North Dakota
- Ohio
- South Dakota
- Wisconsin

Southwest
- Arizona
- New Mexico
- Oklahoma
- Texas

Rockies
- Colorado
- Montana
- Utah
- Wyoming

West
- American Samoa
- California
- Guam
- Hawaii
- Nevada

Pacific NW
- Alaska
- Idaho
- Oregon
- Washington

US National Parks

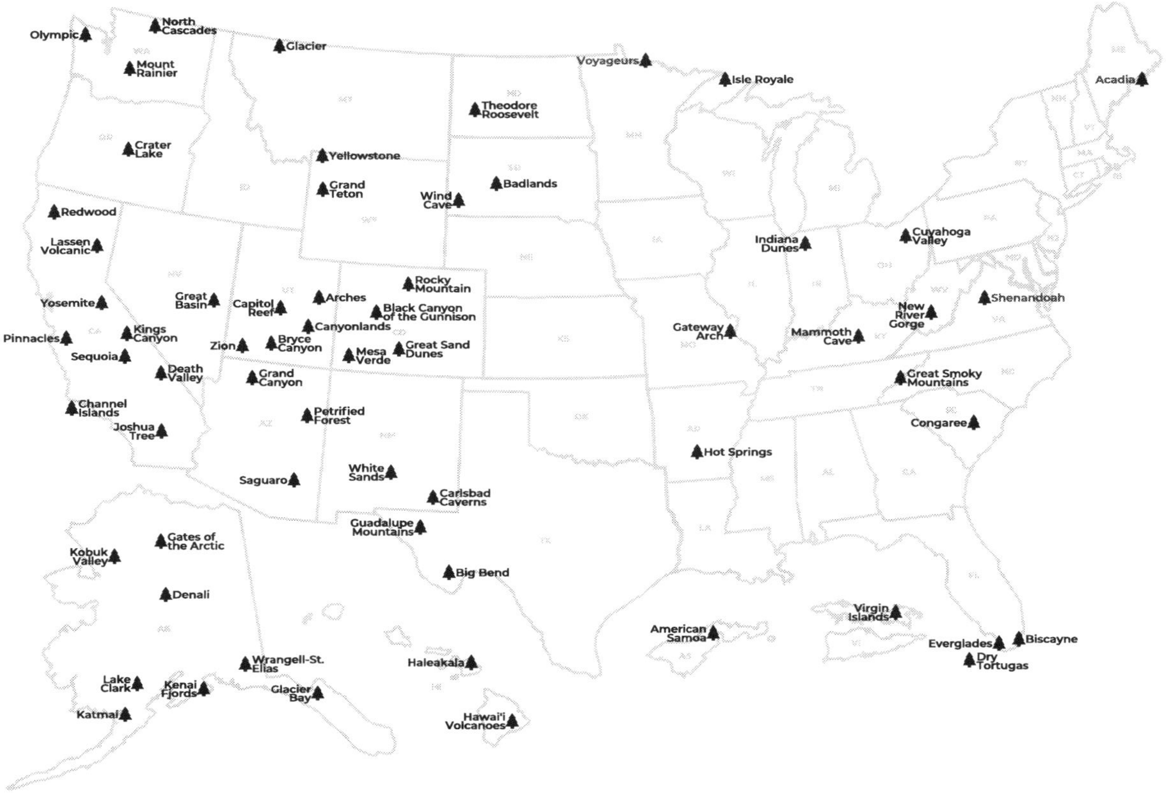

National Parks by State

Alaska
- Denali
- Gates of the Arctic
- Glacier Bay
- Katmai
- Kenai Fjords
- Kobuk Valley
- Lake Clark
- Wrangell-St. Elias

American Samoa
- American Samoa

Arizona
- Grand Canyon
- Petrified Forest
- Saguaro

Arkansas
- Hot Springs

California
- Channel Islands
- Death Valley[1]
- Joshua Tree
- Kings Canyon
- Lassen Volcanic
- Pinnacles
- Redwood
- Sequoia
- Yosemite

Colorado
- Black Canyon of the Gunnison
- Great Sand Dunes
- Mesa Verde
- Rocky Mountain

Florida
- Biscayne
- Dry Tortugas
- Everglades

Hawaii
- Haleakala
- Hawai'i Volcanoes

Kentucky
- Mammoth Cave

Indiana
- Indiana Dunes

Maine
- Acadia

Michigan
- Isle Royale

Minnesota
- Voyageurs

Missouri
- Gateway Arch

Montana
- Glacier

Nevada
- Great Basin

New Mexico
- Carlsbad Caverns
- White Sands

North Dakota
- Theodore Roosevelt

Ohio
- Cuyahoga Valley

Oregon
- Crater Lake

South Carolina
- Congaree

South Dakota
- Badlands
- Wind Cave

Tennessee/ North Carolina
- Great Smoky Mountains

Texas
- Big Bend
- Guadalupe Mountains

Utah
- Arches
- Bryce Canyon
- Canyonlands
- Capitol Reef
- Zion

Virgin Islands
- Virgin Islands

Virginia
- Shenandoah

Washington
- Mount Rainier
- North Cascades
- Olympic

West Virginia
- New River Gorge

Wyoming
- Grand Teton
- Yellowstone[2]

Notes:
1 - Death Valley has a small section in Nevada.
2 - Yellowstone has sections in Idaho and Montana.

Northeast

Connecticut ~ Delaware ~ District of Columbia ~ Maine ~ Maryland ~ Massachusetts ~ New Hampshire ~ New Jersey ~ New York ~ Pennsylvania ~ Rhode Island ~ Vermont

Northeast Units by State

Connecticut
- Weir Farm NHP

Delaware
- First State NHP[1]

District of Columbia
- Belmont-Paul Women's Equality NM
- Carter G. Woodson Home NHS
- Constitution Gardens
- Dwight D. Eisenhower Memorial
- Ford's Theatre NHS
- Franklin D. Roosevelt Memorial
- Fredrick Douglass NHS
- George Washington Memorial Parkway[2]
- Korean War Veterans Memorial
- Lincoln Memorial
- Lyndon Baines Johnson Memorial Grove on the Potomac Memorial
- Martin Luther King, Jr Memorial
- Mary McLeod Bethune Council House NHS
- National Capital Park - East
- National Mall and Memorial Park
- Pennsylvania Avenue NHS
- Rock Creek Park
- Theodore Roosevelt Island

District of Columbia (cont.)
- Thomas Jefferson Memorial
- Vietnam Veterans Memorial
- Washington Monument
- White House and President's Park
- World War I Memorial
- World War II Memorial

Maine
- Acadia NP
- Katahdin Woods and Waters NM
- Saint Croix Island IHS

Maryland
- Antietam NB
- Assateague Island NS[3]
- Catoctin Mountain Park
- Chesapeake and Ohio Canal NHP[3]
- Clara Barton NHS
- Fort McHenry NM & HS
- Fort Washington Park
- Greenbelt Park
- Hampton NHS
- Harriet Tubman Underground Railroad NHP
- Monocacy NB
- Piscataway Park
- Potomac Heritage NST[4]
- Thomas Stone NHS

Massachusetts
- Adams NHP
- Boston NHP
- Boston African American NHS
- Boston Harbor Islands NRA
- Cape Cod NS
- Frederick Law Olmsted NHS
- John F. Kennedy NHS
- Longfellow House–Washington's Headquarters NHS
- Lowell NHP
- Minute Man NHP
- New Bedford Whaling NHP
- Salem Maritime NHS
- Saugus Iron Works NHS
- Springfield Armory NHS

New Hampshire
- Saint-Gaudens NHP

Notes:
1 - Also located in Pennsylvania.

2 - Also located in Maryland and Virginia.

3 - Also located in DC and West Virginia.

4 - Also located in Pennsylvania, DC, and Virginia.

New Jersey

- Delaware Water Gap NRA[1]
- Great Egg Harbor SRR
- Morristown NHP
- Paterson Great Falls NHP
- Thomas Edison NHP

New York

- African Burial Ground NM
- Castle Clinton NM
- Eleanor Roosevelt NHS
- Federal Hall NMEM
- Fire Island NS
- Fort Stanwix NM
- Gateway NRA[2]
- General Grant NMEM
- Governors Island NM
- Hamilton Grange NMEM
- Harriet Tubman NHP
- Home of Franklin D. Roosevelt NHS
- Martin Van Buren NHS
- Sagamore Hill NHS
- Saint Paul's Church NHS
- Saratoga NHP
- Statue of Liberty NM[2]
- Stonewall NM
- Theodore Roosevelt Birthplace NHS
- Theodore Roosevelt Inaugural NHS
- Vanderbilt Mansion NHS
- Women's Rights NHP

Pennsylvania

- Allegheny Portage Railroad NHS
- Delaware NSR[3]
- Edgar Allan Poe NHS
- Eisenhower NHS
- Flight 93 NMEM
- Fort Necessity NB
- Friendship Hill NHS
- Gettysburg NMP
- Hopewell Furnace NHS
- Independence NHP
- Johnstown Flood NMEM
- Steamtown NHS
- Thaddeus Kosciuszko NMEM
- Upper Delaware SRR
- Valley Forge NHP

Rhode Island

- Blackstone River Valley NHP[4]
- Roger Williams NMEM

Vermont

- Marsh-Billings-Rockefeller NHP

Georgia to Maine

- Appalachian NST

Notes:

1 - Also located in Pennsylvania.
2 - Also located in New Jersey.
3 - Also located in New Jersey and New York.
4 - Also located in Massachusetts.

Acadia
National Park
EST. 1919 — 49,071 ACRES — 44° 21' 0" N, 68° 12' 36" W

DATE(S) I VISITED:

WHO I WENT WITH:

Sticker

SIGHTS & WILDLIFE

MY FAVORITE MEMORIES

PASSPORT STAMPS

Adams
National Historical Park

EST. 1946 — 23.82 ACRES — 42° 15' 23" N, 71° 0' 41" W

MA

DATE(S) I VISITED:

WHO I WENT WITH:

Sticker

SIGHTS & WILDLIFE

MY FAVORITE MEMORIES

PASSPORT STAMPS

African Burial Ground
National Monument

NY

EST. 2006 — 0.35 ACRES — 40° 42' 52"N 74° 00' 16"W

DATE(S) I VISITED:

WHO I WENT WITH:

Sticker

SIGHTS & WILDLIFE

MY FAVORITE MEMORIES

PASSPORT STAMPS

Allegheny Portage Railroad
National Historic Site

PA

EST. 1964 — 1,284.27 ACRES — 40° 27' 15" N, 78° 32' 25" W

DATE(S) I VISITED:

Sticker

WHO I WENT WITH:

SIGHTS & WILDLIFE

MY FAVORITE MEMORIES

PASSPORT STAMPS

Antietam
National Battlefield

 MD

EST. 1890 — 3,228.89 ACRES — 39° 28' 13" N, 77° 44' 17" W

DATE(S) I VISITED:

Sticker

WHO I WENT WITH:

SIGHTS & WILDLIFE

MY FAVORITE MEMORIES

PASSPORT STAMPS

Appalachian
National Scenic Trail

GA, NC, TN,
VA, WV, MD,
PA, NJ, NY,
CT, MA, VT,
NH, & ME

EST. 1923 — 2,200 miles ACRES — Georgia to Maine

DATE(S) I VISITED:

WHO I WENT WITH:

Sticker

SIGHTS & WILDLIFE

MY FAVORITE MEMORIES

PASSPORT STAMPS

Assateague Island
National Seashore

MD & VA

EST. 1965 — 41,346.50 ACRES — 38° 5' 0" N, 75° 12' 30" W

DATE(S) I VISITED:

Sticker

WHO I WENT WITH:

SIGHTS & WILDLIFE

MY FAVORITE MEMORIES

PASSPORT STAMPS

Belmont-Paul Women's Equality
National Monument

DC

EST. 2016 — 0.34 ACRES — 38° 53' 31" N, 77° 0' 13" W

DATE(S) I VISITED:

Sticker

WHO I WENT WITH:

SIGHTS & WILDLIFE

MY FAVORITE MEMORIES

PASSPORT STAMPS

Blackstone River Valley
National Historical Park

RI & MA

EST. 2014 — 1,489.00 ACRES — 41° 52' 39" N, 71° 22' 57" W

DATE(S) I VISITED:

WHO I WENT WITH:

Sticker

SIGHTS & WILDLIFE

MY FAVORITE MEMORIES

PASSPORT STAMPS

Boston
National Historical Park

EST. 1974 — 43.82 ACRES — 42° 21' 36" N, 71° 3' 23" W

DATE(S) I VISITED:

Sticker

WHO I WENT WITH:

SIGHTS & WILDLIFE

MY FAVORITE MEMORIES

PASSPORT STAMPS

19

Boston African American
National Historic Site

 MA

EST. 1980 — 0.59 ACRES — 42° 21' 36" N, 71° 3' 53" W

DATE(S) I VISITED:

Sticker

WHO I WENT WITH:

SIGHTS & WILDLIFE

MY FAVORITE MEMORIES

PASSPORT STAMPS

Boston Harbor Islands
National Recreation Area

MA

EST. 1996 — 1,482.31 ACRES — 42° 19' 7" N, 70° 56' 45" W

DATE(S) I VISITED:

Sticker

WHO I WENT WITH:

SIGHTS & WILDLIFE

MY FAVORITE MEMORIES

PASSPORT STAMPS

Cape Cod
National Seashore

EST. 1961 — 43,608.39 ACRES — 41° 50' 14" N, 69° 58' 22" W

DATE(S) I VISITED:

WHO I WENT WITH:

Sticker

SIGHTS & WILDLIFE

MY FAVORITE MEMORIES

PASSPORT STAMPS

Carter G. Woodson Home
National Historic Site

DC

EST. 2006 — 0.15 ACRES — 38° 54' 36" N, 77° 1' 27" W

DATE(S) I VISITED:

Sticker

WHO I WENT WITH:

SIGHTS & WILDLIFE

MY FAVORITE MEMORIES

PASSPORT STAMPS

23

Castle Clinton
National Monument

EST. 1946 — 1 ACRES — 40° 42' 12.6" N, 74° 1' 0.48" W

NY

DATE(S) I VISITED:

WHO I WENT WITH:

Sticker

SIGHTS & WILDLIFE

MY FAVORITE MEMORIES

PASSPORT STAMPS

Catoctin Mountain Park

MD

EST. 1954 — 6,154 ACRES — 39° 38' 4" N, 77° 27' 0" W

DATE(S) I VISITED:

WHO I WENT WITH:

Sticker

SIGHTS & WILDLIFE

MY FAVORITE MEMORIES

PASSPORT STAMPS

Chesapeake and Ohio Canal
National Historical Park

MD, DC, & WV

EST. 1961 — 19,617.37 ACRES — 38° 53' 59" N, 77° 3' 28" W

DATE(S) I VISITED:

Sticker

WHO I WENT WITH:

SIGHTS & WILDLIFE

MY FAVORITE MEMORIES

PASSPORT STAMPS

Clara Barton
National Historic Site

EST. 1974 — 8.59 ACRES — 38° 58' 1" N, 77° 8' 27" W

MD

Sticker

DATE(S) I VISITED:

WHO I WENT WITH:

SIGHTS & WILDLIFE

MY FAVORITE MEMORIES

PASSPORT STAMPS

Constitution Gardens

EST. 1976 — 39.23 ACRES — 38° 53' 27" N, 77° 2' 39" W

DATE(S) I VISITED:

Sticker

WHO I WENT WITH:

SIGHTS & WILDLIFE

MY FAVORITE MEMORIES

PASSPORT STAMPS

Delaware
National Scenic River

PA, NY,
& NJ

EST. 1965 — 1,973.33 ACRES — 41° 9' 13.72" N, 74° 54' 49.97" W

DATE(S) I VISITED:

Sticker

WHO I WENT WITH:

SIGHTS & WILDLIFE

MY FAVORITE MEMORIES

PASSPORT STAMPS

Delaware Water Gap
National Recreation Area

NJ & PA

EST. 1965 — 68,708.88 ACRES — 41° 9' 13.72" N, 74° 54' 49.97" W

DATE(S) I VISITED:

Sticker

WHO I WENT WITH:

SIGHTS & WILDLIFE

MY FAVORITE MEMORIES

PASSPORT STAMPS

Dwight D. Eisenhower
Memorial

EST. 2020 — 3.39 ACRES — 38° 53' 13.85" N, 77° 1' 7.58" W

DATE(S) I VISITED:

Sticker

WHO I WENT WITH:

SIGHTS & WILDLIFE

MY FAVORITE MEMORIES

PASSPORT STAMPS

Edgar Allan Poe
National Historic Site

EST. 1978 — 0.52 ACRES — 39° 57' 42" N, 75° 9' 1" W

DATE(S) I VISITED:

Sticker

WHO I WENT WITH:

SIGHTS & WILDLIFE

MY FAVORITE MEMORIES

PASSPORT STAMPS

Eisenhower
National Historic Site

EST. 1980 — 690.46 ACRES — 39° 47' 36" N, 77° 15' 48" W

PA

DATE(S) I VISITED:

WHO I WENT WITH:

Sticker

SIGHTS & WILDLIFE

MY FAVORITE MEMORIES

PASSPORT STAMPS

Eleanor Roosevelt
National Historic Site

EST. 1977 — 180.5 ACRES — 41° 45' 47" N, 73° 53' 56" W

DATE(S) I VISITED:

Sticker

WHO I WENT WITH:

SIGHTS & WILDLIFE

MY FAVORITE MEMORIES

PASSPORT STAMPS

Federal Hall
National Memorial

NY

EST. 1955 — 0.45 ACRES — 40° 42' 26" N, 74° 0' 37" W

DATE(S) I VISITED:

WHO I WENT WITH:

Sticker

SIGHTS & WILDLIFE

MY FAVORITE MEMORIES

PASSPORT STAMPS

Fire Island
National Seashore

EST. 1964 — 19,580.65 ACRES — 40° 41' 47" N, 72° 58' 58" W

DATE(S) I VISITED:

WHO I WENT WITH:

Sticker

SIGHTS & WILDLIFE

MY FAVORITE MEMORIES

PASSPORT STAMPS

First State
National Historical Park

EST. 2013 — 1,409.22 ACRES — 39° 39' 53" N, 75° 33' 55" W

DATE(S) I VISITED:

Sticker

WHO I WENT WITH:

SIGHTS & WILDLIFE

MY FAVORITE MEMORIES

PASSPORT STAMPS

Flight 93
National Memorial

EST. 2002 — 2,262.65 ACRES — 40° 3' 24" N, 78° 54' 21" W

DATE(S) I VISITED:

Sticker

WHO I WENT WITH:

SIGHTS & WILDLIFE

MY FAVORITE MEMORIES

PASSPORT STAMPS

Ford's Theatre
National Historic Site

EST. 1932 — 0.3 ACRES — 38° 53' 48" N, 77° 1' 33" W

DATE(S) I VISITED:

WHO I WENT WITH:

Sticker

SIGHTS & WILDLIFE

MY FAVORITE MEMORIES

PASSPORT STAMPS

MD

Fort McHenry National
Monument and Historic Shrine

EST. 1939 — 43.26 ACRES — 39° 15' 47" N, 76° 34' 48" W

DATE(S) I VISITED:

Sticker

WHO I WENT WITH:

SIGHTS & WILDLIFE

MY FAVORITE MEMORIES

PASSPORT STAMPS

Fort Necessity
National Battlefield

EST. 1931 — 902.8 ACRES — 39° 48' 55" N, 79° 35' 22" W

PA

DATE(S) I VISITED:

WHO I WENT WITH:

Sticker

SIGHTS & WILDLIFE

MY FAVORITE MEMORIES

PASSPORT STAMPS

Fort Stanwix
National Monument

EST. 1935 — 15.52 ACRES — 43° 12' 38" N, 75° 27' 18.9" W

DATE(S) I VISITED:

Sticker

WHO I WENT WITH:

SIGHTS & WILDLIFE

MY FAVORITE MEMORIES

PASSPORT STAMPS

Fort Washington Park

MD

EST. 1946 — 345.05 ACRES — 38° 42' 39" N, 77° 1' 59" W

DATE(S) I VISITED:

WHO I WENT WITH:

Sticker

SIGHTS & WILDLIFE

MY FAVORITE MEMORIES

PASSPORT STAMPS

Franklin D. Roosevelt
Memorial

EST. 1997 — 8.14 ACRES — 38° 53' 2" N, 77° 2' 40" W

DATE(S) I VISITED:

Sticker

WHO I WENT WITH:

SIGHTS & WILDLIFE

MY FAVORITE MEMORIES

PASSPORT STAMPS

Frederick Douglass
National Historic Site

EST. 1988 — 8.57 ACRES — 38° 51' 48" N, 76° 59' 7" W

DATE(S) I VISITED:

WHO I WENT WITH:

Sticker

SIGHTS & WILDLIFE

MY FAVORITE MEMORIES

PASSPORT STAMPS

Frederick Law Olmsted
National Historic Site

EST. 1979 — 7.21 ACRES — 42° 19' 30" N, 71° 7' 56" W

DATE(S) I VISITED:

Sticker

WHO I WENT WITH:

SIGHTS & WILDLIFE

MY FAVORITE MEMORIES

PASSPORT STAMPS

Friendship Hill
National Historic Site

EST. 1978 — 674.56 ACRES — 39° 46' 40" N, 79° 55' 45" W

DATE(S) I VISITED:

WHO I WENT WITH:

Sticker

SIGHTS & WILDLIFE

MY FAVORITE MEMORIES

PASSPORT STAMPS

Gateway
National Recreation Area

NY & NJ

EST. 1972 — 26,606.63 ACRES — 40° 27' 14.4" N, 73° 59' 49.16" W

DATE(S) I VISITED:

WHO I WENT WITH:

Sticker

SIGHTS & WILDLIFE

MY FAVORITE MEMORIES

PASSPORT STAMPS

General Grant
National Memorial

EST. 1958 — 0.76 ACRES — 40° 48' 48" N, 73° 57' 47" W

DATE(S) I VISITED:

WHO I WENT WITH:

Sticker

SIGHTS & WILDLIFE

MY FAVORITE MEMORIES

PASSPORT STAMPS

George Washington Memorial
Parkway

EST. 1930 — 24.9 mi ACRES — 38° 51' 40.4028"N, 77° 2' 43.2384" W

DC, MD, & VA

DATE(S) I VISITED:

Sticker

WHO I WENT WITH:

SIGHTS & WILDLIFE

MY FAVORITE MEMORIES

PASSPORT STAMPS

Gettysburg
National Military Park

EST. 1895 — 6,032.07 ACRES — 39° 48' 31" N, 77° 14' 12" W

Sticker

DATE(S) I VISITED:

WHO I WENT WITH:

SIGHTS & WILDLIFE

MY FAVORITE MEMORIES

PASSPORT STAMPS

Governors Island
National Monument

EST. 2001 — 22.91 ACRES — 40° 41' 29" N, 74° 0' 58" W

DATE(S) I VISITED:

Sticker

WHO I WENT WITH:

SIGHTS & WILDLIFE

MY FAVORITE MEMORIES

PASSPORT STAMPS

Great Egg Harbor
Scenic and Recreational River

NJ

EST. 1992 — 43,311.42 ACRES — 39°18'9.00" N -74°38'35.39" W

Sticker

DATE(S) I VISITED:

WHO I WENT WITH:

SIGHTS & WILDLIFE

MY FAVORITE MEMORIES

PASSPORT STAMPS

Greenbelt Park

EST. 1950 — 1,175.99 ACRES — 38° 59' 0" N, 76° 53' 52" W

DATE(S) I VISITED:

WHO I WENT WITH:

Sticker

SIGHTS & WILDLIFE

MY FAVORITE MEMORIES

PASSPORT STAMPS

Hamilton Grange
National Memorial

NY

EST. 1962 — 1.75 ACRES — 40° 49' 17" N, 73° 56' 50" W

DATE(S) I VISITED:

WHO I WENT WITH:

Sticker

SIGHTS & WILDLIFE

MY FAVORITE MEMORIES

PASSPORT STAMPS

Hampton
National Historic Site

EST. 1948 — 62.04 ACRES — 39° 24' 58" N, 76° 35' 15" W

DATE(S) I VISITED:

WHO I WENT WITH:

Sticker

SIGHTS & WILDLIFE

MY FAVORITE MEMORIES

PASSPORT STAMPS

Harriet Tubman
National Historical Park

 NY

EST. 2017 — 31.5 ACRES — 42° 54' 39.97" N, 76° 34' 4.01" W

DATE(S) I VISITED:

WHO I WENT WITH:

Sticker

SIGHTS & WILDLIFE

MY FAVORITE MEMORIES

PASSPORT STAMPS

Harriet Tubman Underground Railroad
National Historical Park

MD

EST. 2014 — 480 ACRES — 38° 26' 53.88" N, 76° 8' 19.32" W

DATE(S) I VISITED:

Sticker

WHO I WENT WITH:

SIGHTS & WILDLIFE

MY FAVORITE MEMORIES

PASSPORT STAMPS

Home of Franklin D. Roosevelt
National Historic Site

NY

EST. 1944 — 838.43 ACRES — 41° 46' 2" N, 73° 56' 8" W

DATE(S) I VISITED:

Sticker

WHO I WENT WITH:

SIGHTS & WILDLIFE

MY FAVORITE MEMORIES

PASSPORT STAMPS

Hopewell Furnace
National Historic Site

EST. 1938 — 848.06 ACRES — 40° 11' 55" N, 75° 46' 32" W

DATE(S) I VISITED:

Sticker

WHO I WENT WITH:

SIGHTS & WILDLIFE

MY FAVORITE MEMORIES

PASSPORT STAMPS

Independence
National Historical Park

EST. 1948 — 44.87 ACRES — 39° 56' 52" N, 75° 8' 53" W

PA

Sticker

DATE(S) I VISITED:

WHO I WENT WITH:

SIGHTS & WILDLIFE

MY FAVORITE MEMORIES

PASSPORT STAMPS

John F. Kennedy
National Historic Site

EST. 1967 — 0.09 ACRES — 42° 20' 49" N, 71° 7' 24" W

DATE(S) I VISITED:

WHO I WENT WITH:

Sticker

SIGHTS & WILDLIFE

MY FAVORITE MEMORIES

PASSPORT STAMPS

Johnstown Flood
National Memorial

 PA

EST. 1964 — 177.76 ACRES — 40° 20' 44" N, 78° 46' 43" W

DATE(S) I VISITED:

Sticker

WHO I WENT WITH:

SIGHTS & WILDLIFE

MY FAVORITE MEMORIES

PASSPORT STAMPS

Katahdin Woods and Waters
National Monument

ME

EST. 2016 — 87,564.27 ACRES — 45° 58' 13.3" N, 68° 37' 9.61" W

DATE(S) I VISITED:

Sticker

WHO I WENT WITH:

SIGHTS & WILDLIFE

MY FAVORITE MEMORIES

PASSPORT STAMPS

Korean War Veterans
Memorial

EST. 1995 — 1.56 ACRES — 38° 53' 16" N, 77° 2' 50" W

DATE(S) I VISITED:

WHO I WENT WITH:

Sticker

SIGHTS & WILDLIFE

MY FAVORITE MEMORIES

PASSPORT STAMPS

Lincoln
Memorial

EST. 1922 — 7.29 ACRES — 38° 53' 21.4" N, 77° 3' 0.5" W

DATE(S) I VISITED:

Sticker

WHO I WENT WITH:

SIGHTS & WILDLIFE

MY FAVORITE MEMORIES

PASSPORT STAMPS

Longfellow House–Washington's Headquarters
National Historic Site

MA

EST. 1972 — 1.98 ACRES — 42° 22' 36" N, 71° 7' 35" W

DATE(S) I VISITED:

Sticker

WHO I WENT WITH:

SIGHTS & WILDLIFE

MY FAVORITE MEMORIES

PASSPORT STAMPS

Lowell
National Historical Park

EST. 1978 — 143.37 ACRES — 42° 38' 48" N, 71° 18' 37" W

DATE(S) I VISITED:

Sticker

WHO I WENT WITH:

SIGHTS & WILDLIFE

MY FAVORITE MEMORIES

PASSPORT STAMPS

Lyndon Baines Johnson Memorial
Grove on the Potomac Memorial

DC

EST. 1973 — 17 ACRES — 38° 52' 43" N, 77° 3' 5" W

DATE(S) I VISITED:

Sticker

WHO I WENT WITH:

SIGHTS & WILDLIFE

MY FAVORITE MEMORIES

PASSPORT STAMPS

69

Marsh-Billings-Rockefeller
National Historical Park

VT

EST. 1992 — 643.07 ACRES — 43° 37' 52.49" N, 72° 31' 45.68" W

DATE(S) I VISITED:

Sticker

WHO I WENT WITH:

SIGHTS & WILDLIFE

MY FAVORITE MEMORIES

PASSPORT STAMPS

Martin Luther King, Jr.
Memorial

EST. 2011 — 2.74 ACRES — 38° 53' 10" N, 77° 2' 39" W

DATE(S) I VISITED:

WHO I WENT WITH:

Sticker

SIGHTS & WILDLIFE

MY FAVORITE MEMORIES

PASSPORT STAMPS

Martin Van Buren
National Historic Site

EST. 1974 — 284.93 ACRES — 42° 22' 10.94" N, 73° 42' 15.14" W

DATE(S) I VISITED:

WHO I WENT WITH:

Sticker

SIGHTS & WILDLIFE

MY FAVORITE MEMORIES

PASSPORT STAMPS

Mary McLeod Bethune Council House
National Historic Site

DC

EST. 1982 — 0.07 ACRES — 38° 54' 28" N, 77° 1' 49" W

DATE(S) I VISITED:

WHO I WENT WITH:

Sticker

SIGHTS & WILDLIFE

MY FAVORITE MEMORIES

PASSPORT STAMPS

Minute Man
National Historical Park

EST. 1959 — 1,027.76 ACRES — 42° 27' 11" N, 71° 17' 55" W

DATE(S) I VISITED:

Sticker

WHO I WENT WITH:

SIGHTS & WILDLIFE

MY FAVORITE MEMORIES

PASSPORT STAMPS

Monocacy
National Battlefield

MD

EST. 1934 — 1,646.88 ACRES — 39° 22' 16.14" N, 77° 23' 31.49" W

DATE(S) I VISITED:

WHO I WENT WITH:

Sticker

SIGHTS & WILDLIFE

MY FAVORITE MEMORIES

PASSPORT STAMPS

Morristown
National Historical Park

EST. 1933 — 1,710.72 ACRES — 40° 47' 47" N, 74° 28' 0" W

DATE(S) I VISITED:

Sticker

WHO I WENT WITH:

SIGHTS & WILDLIFE

MY FAVORITE MEMORIES

PASSPORT STAMPS

National Capital Park - East

EST. 1965 — 8,703.64 ACRES — 38° 52' 42" N, 76° 58' 9" W

DATE(S) I VISITED:

Sticker

WHO I WENT WITH:

SIGHTS & WILDLIFE

MY FAVORITE MEMORIES

PASSPORT STAMPS

National Mall
And Memorial Park

EST. 1965 — 155.84 ACRES — 38° 53' 24" N, 77° 1' 22" W

DATE(S) I VISITED:

Sticker

WHO I WENT WITH:

SIGHTS & WILDLIFE

MY FAVORITE MEMORIES

PASSPORT STAMPS

New Bedford Whaling
National Historical Park

MA

EST. 1996 — 34 ACRES — 41° 38' 8" N, 70° 55' 24" W

DATE(S) I VISITED:

WHO I WENT WITH:

Sticker

SIGHTS & WILDLIFE

MY FAVORITE MEMORIES

PASSPORT STAMPS

Paterson Great Falls
National Historical Park

EST. 2009 — 51.33 ACRES — 40° 54' 58" N, 74° 10' 54" W

DATE(S) I VISITED:

Sticker

WHO I WENT WITH:

SIGHTS & WILDLIFE

MY FAVORITE MEMORIES

PASSPORT STAMPS

Pennsylvania Avenue
National Historic Site

EST. 1965 — 17.61 ACRES — 38° 53' 37" N, 77° 1' 26" W

Sticker

DATE(S) I VISITED:

WHO I WENT WITH:

SIGHTS & WILDLIFE

MY FAVORITE MEMORIES

PASSPORT STAMPS

Piscataway Park

EST. 1961 — 4,616.31 ACRES — 38° 40' 43" N, 77° 5' 34" W

DATE(S) I VISITED:

Sticker

WHO I WENT WITH:

SIGHTS & WILDLIFE

MY FAVORITE MEMORIES

PASSPORT STAMPS

Potomac Heritage
National Scenic Trail

MD, DC, PA, & VA

EST. 1983 — 710 mi ACRES — 38° 42' 36.03" N, 77° 3' 40.87" W

DATE(S) I VISITED:

WHO I WENT WITH:

Sticker

SIGHTS & WILDLIFE

MY FAVORITE MEMORIES

PASSPORT STAMPS

Rock Creek Park

EST. 1890 — 1,755.21 ACRES — 38° 57' 27" N, 77° 2' 42" W

DATE(S) I VISITED:

Sticker

WHO I WENT WITH:

SIGHTS & WILDLIFE

MY FAVORITE MEMORIES

PASSPORT STAMPS

Roger Williams
National Memorial

EST. 1965 — 4.56 ACRES — 41° 49' 49.37" N, 71° 24' 39.2" W

DATE(S) I VISITED:

Sticker

WHO I WENT WITH:

SIGHTS & WILDLIFE

MY FAVORITE MEMORIES

PASSPORT STAMPS

Sagamore Hill
National Historic Site

EST. 1962 — 83.02 ACRES — 40° 53' 8" N, 73° 29' 51" W

DATE(S) I VISITED:

WHO I WENT WITH:

Sticker

SIGHTS & WILDLIFE

MY FAVORITE MEMORIES

PASSPORT STAMPS

Saint Croix Island
International Historic Site

EST. 1949 — 6.5 ACRES — 45° 7' 42" N, 67° 8' 0" W

ME

DATE(S) I VISITED:

WHO I WENT WITH:

Sticker

SIGHTS & WILDLIFE

MY FAVORITE MEMORIES

PASSPORT STAMPS

Saint Paul's Church
National Historic Site

EST. 1943 — 6.13 ACRES — 40° 53' 34" N, 73° 49' 33" W

DATE(S) I VISITED:

Sticker

WHO I WENT WITH:

SIGHTS & WILDLIFE

MY FAVORITE MEMORIES

PASSPORT STAMPS

Saint-Gaudens
National Historical Park

EST. 1964 — 190.75 ACRES — 43° 30' 3" N, 72° 22' 5" W

DATE(S) I VISITED:

WHO I WENT WITH:

Sticker

SIGHTS & WILDLIFE

MY FAVORITE MEMORIES

PASSPORT STAMPS

Salem Maritime
National Historic Site

EST. 1938 — 9.02 ACRES — 42° 31' 14" N, 70° 53' 14" W

DATE(S) I VISITED:

WHO I WENT WITH:

Sticker

SIGHTS & WILDLIFE

MY FAVORITE MEMORIES

PASSPORT STAMPS

Saratoga
National Historical Park

EST. 1938 — 3,607.59 ACRES — 42° 59' 56" N, 73° 38' 15" W

DATE(S) I VISITED:

Sticker

WHO I WENT WITH:

SIGHTS & WILDLIFE

MY FAVORITE MEMORIES

PASSPORT STAMPS

Saugus Iron Works
National Historic Site

EST. 1968 — 8.51 ACRES — 42° 28' 7" N, 71° 0' 32" W

DATE(S) I VISITED:

Sticker

WHO I WENT WITH:

SIGHTS & WILDLIFE

MY FAVORITE MEMORIES

PASSPORT STAMPS

Springfield Armory
National Historic Site

 MA

EST. 1968 — 54.93 ACRES — 42° 6' 29" N, 72° 34' 54" W

DATE(S) I VISITED:

WHO I WENT WITH:

Sticker

SIGHTS & WILDLIFE

MY FAVORITE MEMORIES

PASSPORT STAMPS

Statue of Liberty
National Monument

NY & NJ

EST. 1924 — 58.38 ACRES — 40° 41' 39" N, 74° 2' 35" W

DATE(S) I VISITED:

Sticker

WHO I WENT WITH:

SIGHTS & WILDLIFE

MY FAVORITE MEMORIES

PASSPORT STAMPS

Steamtown
National Historic Site

EST. 1986 — 62.48 ACRES — 41° 24' 26.39" N, 75° 40' 16.75" W

PA

DATE(S) I VISITED:

Sticker

WHO I WENT WITH:

SIGHTS & WILDLIFE

MY FAVORITE MEMORIES

PASSPORT STAMPS

Stonewall
National Monument

EST. 2016 — 7.7 ACRES — 40° 44' 1.94" N, 74° 0' 7.83" W

DATE(S) I VISITED:

Sticker

WHO I WENT WITH:

SIGHTS & WILDLIFE

MY FAVORITE MEMORIES

PASSPORT STAMPS

Thaddeus Kosciuszko
National Memorial

EST. 1972 — 0.02 ACRES — 39° 56' 36.38" N, 75° 8' 50.2" W

DATE(S) I VISITED:

Sticker

WHO I WENT WITH:

SIGHTS & WILDLIFE

MY FAVORITE MEMORIES

PASSPORT STAMPS

Theodore Roosevelt Birthplace
National Historic Site

NY

EST. 1963 — 0.11 ACRES — 40° 44' 19.7" N, 73° 59' 20" W

DATE(S) I VISITED:

Sticker

WHO I WENT WITH:

SIGHTS & WILDLIFE

MY FAVORITE MEMORIES

PASSPORT STAMPS

Theodore Roosevelt Inaugural
National Historic Site

NY

EST. 1966 — 1.18 ACRES — 42° 54' 5.3" N, 78° 52' 20.7" W

DATE(S) I VISITED:

Sticker

WHO I WENT WITH:

SIGHTS & WILDLIFE

MY FAVORITE MEMORIES

PASSPORT STAMPS

Theodore Roosevelt Island

 DC

EST. 1932 — 88.5 ACRES — 38° 53' 50" N, 77° 3' 51" W

DATE(S) I VISITED:

WHO I WENT WITH:

Sticker

SIGHTS & WILDLIFE

MY FAVORITE MEMORIES

PASSPORT STAMPS

Thomas Edison
National Historical Park

EST. 1962 — 21.25 ACRES — 40° 47' 1" N, 74° 14' 1" W

NJ

DATE(S) I VISITED:

WHO I WENT WITH:

Sticker

SIGHTS & WILDLIFE

MY FAVORITE MEMORIES

PASSPORT STAMPS

Thomas Jefferson
Memorial

EST. 1943 — 18.36 ACRES — 38° 52' 53" N, 77° 2' 12" W

DATE(S) I VISITED:

WHO I WENT WITH:

Sticker

SIGHTS & WILDLIFE

MY FAVORITE MEMORIES

PASSPORT STAMPS

Thomas Stone
National Historic Site

MD

EST. 1999 — 328.25 ACRES — 42° 13' 33" N, 73° 51' 43" W

DATE(S) I VISITED:

Sticker

WHO I WENT WITH:

SIGHTS & WILDLIFE

MY FAVORITE MEMORIES

PASSPORT STAMPS

Upper Delaware
Scenic and Recreational River

PA & NY

EST. 1978 — 74,999.56 ACRES — 41° 38' 24.29" N, 75° 3' 30.92" W

DATE(S) I VISITED:

WHO I WENT WITH:

Sticker

SIGHTS & WILDLIFE

MY FAVORITE MEMORIES

PASSPORT STAMPS

Valley Forge
National Historical Park

EST. 1976 — 3,468.54 ACRES — 40° 5' 49" N, 75° 26' 20" W

DATE(S) I VISITED:

Sticker

WHO I WENT WITH:

SIGHTS & WILDLIFE

MY FAVORITE MEMORIES

PASSPORT STAMPS

Vanderbilt Mansion
National Historic Site

EST. 1940 — 211.65 ACRES — 41° 47' 46" N, 73° 56' 31" W

DATE(S) I VISITED:

WHO I WENT WITH:

Sticker

SIGHTS & WILDLIFE

MY FAVORITE MEMORIES

PASSPORT STAMPS

Vietnam Veterans
Memorial

EST. 1982 — 2.18 ACRES — 38° 53' 28" N, 77° 2' 52" W

DATE(S) I VISITED:

WHO I WENT WITH:

Sticker

SIGHTS & WILDLIFE

MY FAVORITE MEMORIES

PASSPORT STAMPS

Washington
Monument

EST. 1888 — 106.01 ACRES — 38° 53' 22" N, 77° 2' 7" W

DATE(S) I VISITED:

WHO I WENT WITH:

Sticker

SIGHTS & WILDLIFE

MY FAVORITE MEMORIES

PASSPORT STAMPS

Weir Farm
National Historical Park

EST. 1990 — 74.2 ACRES — 41° 15' 29.02" N, 73° 27' 16.99" W

DATE(S) I VISITED:

Sticker

WHO I WENT WITH:

SIGHTS & WILDLIFE

MY FAVORITE MEMORIES

PASSPORT STAMPS

White House and President's
Park

EST. 1791 — 18.07 ACRES — 38° 53' 46" N, 77° 2' 12" W

DATE(S) I VISITED:

Sticker

WHO I WENT WITH:

SIGHTS & WILDLIFE

MY FAVORITE MEMORIES

PASSPORT STAMPS

Women's Rights
National Historical Park

EST. 1980 — 7.44 ACRES — 42° 54' 39" N, 76° 48' 5" W

DATE(S) I VISITED:

WHO I WENT WITH:

Sticker

SIGHTS & WILDLIFE

MY FAVORITE MEMORIES

PASSPORT STAMPS

World War I
Memorial

EST. 1981 — 1.39 ACRES — 38° 53' 46" N, 77° 1' 58" W

DATE(S) I VISITED:

Sticker

WHO I WENT WITH:

SIGHTS & WILDLIFE

MY FAVORITE MEMORIES

PASSPORT STAMPS

World War II
Memorial

EST. 2004 — 8.25 ACRES — 38° 53' 22" N, 77° 2' 26" W

DATE(S) I VISITED:

WHO I WENT WITH:

Sticker

SIGHTS & WILDLIFE

MY FAVORITE MEMORIES

PASSPORT STAMPS

_____

_____

EST. _____ — _____ ACRES — ___° ___' ___" N, ___° ___' ___" W

DATE(S) I VISITED:

Sticker

WHO I WENT WITH:

SIGHTS & WILDLIFE

MY FAVORITE MEMORIES

PASSPORT STAMPS

_____

_____

— EST. _____ — _____ ACRES — ___° __' __" N, ___° __' __" W

DATE(S) I VISITED:

WHO I WENT WITH:

Sticker

SIGHTS & WILDLIFE

MY FAVORITE MEMORIES

PASSPORT STAMPS

EST. _____ — _____ ACRES — __° __' __" N, __° __' __" W

DATE(S) I VISITED:

Sticker

WHO I WENT WITH:

SIGHTS & WILDLIFE

MY FAVORITE MEMORIES

PASSPORT STAMPS

_____

_____

_____

EST. _____ — _____ ACRES — ___° ___' ___" N, ___° ___' ___" W

DATE(S) I VISITED:

WHO I WENT WITH:

Sticker

SIGHTS & WILDLIFE

MY FAVORITE MEMORIES

PASSPORT STAMPS

Southeast

**Alabama ~ Florida ~ Georgia ~ Kentucky ~ Louisiana
~ Mississippi ~ North Carolina ~ Puerto Rico ~
South Carolina ~ Tennessee ~ Virgin Islands ~
Virginia ~ West Virginia**

Southeast Units by State

Alabama

- Birmingham Civil Rights NM
- Freedom Riders NM
- Horseshoe Bend NMP
- Little River Canyon NPRES
- Russell Cave NM
- Tuskegee Airmen NHS
- Tuskegee Institute NHS

Florida

- Big Cypress NPRES
- Biscayne NP
- Canaveral NS
- Castillo de San Marcos NM
- De Soto NMEM
- Dry Tortugas NP
- Everglades NP
- Fort Caroline NMEM
- Fort Matanzas NM
- Gulf Islands NS[1]
- Timucuan Ecological and Historic Preserve

Georgia

- Andersonville NHS
- Chattahoochee River NRA
- Chickamauga & Chattanooga NMP[2]
- Cumberland Island NS
- Fort Frederica NM
- Fort Pulaski NM
- Jimmy Carter NHP
- Kennesaw Mountain NBP
- Martin Luther King, Jr. NHP
- Ocmulgee Mounds NHP

Kentucky

- Abraham Lincoln Birthplace NHP
- Camp Nelson Heritage NM
- Fort Donelson NB[2]
- Mammoth Cave NP
- Mill Springs Battlefield NM

Louisiana

- Cane River Creole NHP
- Jean Lafitte NHP & PRES
- New Orleans Jazz NHP
- Poverty Point NM

Mississippi

- Brices Cross Roads NBS
- Medgar and Myrlie Evers Home NM
- Natchez NHP
- Natchez Trace NST[3]
- Natchez Trace Parkway[3]
- Tupelo NB
- Vicksburg NMP[4]

North Carolina

- Blue Ridge Parkway[5]
- Cape Hatteras NS
- Cape Lookout NS
- Carl Sandburg Home NHS
- Fort Raleigh NHS
- Guilford Courthouse NMP
- Moores Creek NB
- Wright Brothers NMEM

Puerto Rico

- San Juan NHS

South Carolina

- Charles Pinckney NHS
- Congaree NP
- Cowpens NB
- Fort Sumter and Fort Moultrie NHP
- Kings Mountain NMP
- Ninety Six NHS
- Reconstruction Era NHP

Notes:

1 - Also located in Mississippi
2 - Also located in Tennessee
3 - Also located in Tennessee and Alabama
4 - Also located in Louisiana
5 - Also located in Virginia
6 - Appalachian NST can Northeast Region found under Georgia to Maine.

Tennessee

- Andrew Johnson NHS
- Big South Fork NR & RA[1]
- Cumberland Gap NHP[2]
- Great Smoky Mountains NP[3]
- Manhattan Project NHP[4]
- Obed WSR
- Shiloh NMP[5]
- Stones River NB

Virgin Islands

- Buck Island Reef NM
- Christiansted NHS
- Salt River Bay NHP & PRES
- Virgin Islands NP
- Virgin Islands Coral Reef NM

Virginia[6]

- Appomattox Court House NHP
- Arlington House, The Robert E. Lee Memorial
- Booker T. Washington NM
- Cedar Creek and Belle Grove NHP
- Colonial NHP
- Fort Monroe NM
- Fredericksburg and Spotsylvania NMP
- George Washington Birthplace NM
- Maggie L. Walker NHS
- Manassas NBP
- Petersburg NB
- Prince William Forest Park
- Richmond NBP
- Shenandoah NP
- Wolf Trap NPPA

West Virginia

- Bluestone NSR
- Gauley River NRA
- Harpers Ferry NHP[7]
- New River Gorge NP & PRES

Notes:

1 - Also located in Kentucky.

2 - Also located in Kentucky and Virginia.

3 - Also located in North Carolina.

4 - Also located in New Mexico and Washington.

5 - Also located in Mississippi

6 - Assateague Island NS, Potomac Heritage NST, and Chesapeake and Ohio Canal NHP can be found in the Northeast Region under Maryland.

7 - Also located in Virginia and Maryland

Abraham Lincoln Birthplace
National Historical Park

KY

EST. 1916 — 344.5 ACRES — 37° 31' 53" N, 85° 44' 10" W

DATE(S) I VISITED:

WHO I WENT WITH:

Sticker

SIGHTS & WILDLIFE

MY FAVORITE MEMORIES

PASSPORT STAMPS

Andersonville
National Historic Site

EST. 1970 — 515.61 ACRES — 32° 11' 54" N, 84° 7' 48" W

GA

DATE(S) I VISITED:

Sticker

WHO I WENT WITH:

SIGHTS & WILDLIFE

MY FAVORITE MEMORIES

PASSPORT STAMPS

Andrew Johnson
National Historic Site

EST. 1942 — 16.68 ACRES — 36° 9' 30" N, 82° 50' 6" W

TN

Sticker

DATE(S) I VISITED:

WHO I WENT WITH:

SIGHTS & WILDLIFE

MY FAVORITE MEMORIES

PASSPORT STAMPS

123

Appomattox Court House
National Historical Park

EST. 1935 — 1,774.60 ACRES — 37° 22' 39" N, 78° 47' 45.6" W

VA

DATE(S) I VISITED:

Sticker

WHO I WENT WITH:

SIGHTS & WILDLIFE

MY FAVORITE MEMORIES

PASSPORT STAMPS

Arlington House, The Robert E. Lee Memorial

VA

EST. 1933 — 17.12 ACRES — 38° 52' 55.75" N, 77° 4' 24.68" W

DATE(S) I VISITED:

WHO I WENT WITH:

Sticker

SIGHTS & WILDLIFE

MY FAVORITE MEMORIES

PASSPORT STAMPS

Big Cypress
National Preserve

EST. 1974 — 720,564.01 ACRES — 25° 51' 32" N, 81° 2' 2" W

FL

DATE(S) I VISITED:

WHO I WENT WITH:

Sticker

SIGHTS & WILDLIFE

MY FAVORITE MEMORIES

PASSPORT STAMPS

Big South Fork
National River and Recreation Area

TN & KY

EST. 1974 — 123,698.72 ACRES — 36° 29' 11.4" N, 84° 41' 54.6" W

DATE(S) I VISITED:

Sticker

WHO I WENT WITH:

SIGHTS & WILDLIFE

MY FAVORITE MEMORIES

PASSPORT STAMPS

Birmingham Civil Rights
National Monument

AL

EST. 2017 — 18.25 ACRES — 33° 30' 55" N, 86° 48' 53" W

DATE(S) I VISITED:

Sticker

WHO I WENT WITH:

SIGHTS & WILDLIFE

MY FAVORITE MEMORIES

PASSPORT STAMPS

Biscayne
National Park

FL

EST. 1980 — 172,971 ACRES — 25° 39' 0" N, 80° 4' 48" W

DATE(S) I VISITED:

Sticker

WHO I WENT WITH:

SIGHTS & WILDLIFE

MY FAVORITE MEMORIES

PASSPORT STAMPS

Blue Ridge
Parkway

 NC & VA

EST. 1963 — 469 mi ACRES — 36° 31' 7" N, 80° 56' 9" W

DATE(S) I VISITED:

Sticker

WHO I WENT WITH:

SIGHTS & WILDLIFE

MY FAVORITE MEMORIES

PASSPORT STAMPS

Bluestone
National Scenic River

EST. 1988 — 4,309.51 ACRES — 37° 32' 30" N, 80° 59' 57" W

DATE(S) I VISITED:

WHO I WENT WITH:

Sticker

SIGHTS & WILDLIFE

MY FAVORITE MEMORIES

PASSPORT STAMPS

Booker T. Washington
National Monument

 VA

EST. 1956 — 239.01 ACRES — 37° 7' 10.58" N, 79° 43' 53.45" W

DATE(S) I VISITED:

Sticker

WHO I WENT WITH:

SIGHTS & WILDLIFE

MY FAVORITE MEMORIES

PASSPORT STAMPS

Brices Cross Roads
National Battlefield Site

EST. 1929 — 1 ACRES — 34° 30' 22" N, 88° 43' 44" W

DATE(S) I VISITED:

WHO I WENT WITH:

Sticker

SIGHTS & WILDLIFE

MY FAVORITE MEMORIES

PASSPORT STAMPS

Buck Island Reef
National Monument

 VI

EST. 1961 — 19,015.47 ACRES — 17° 47' 12.98" N, 64° 37' 8.98" W

DATE(S) I VISITED:

Sticker

WHO I WENT WITH:

SIGHTS & WILDLIFE

MY FAVORITE MEMORIES

PASSPORT STAMPS

Camp Nelson Heritage
National Monument

KY

EST. 2018 — 464.97 ACRES — 37° 47' 16" N, 84° 35' 53" W

DATE(S) I VISITED:

WHO I WENT WITH:

Sticker

SIGHTS & WILDLIFE

MY FAVORITE MEMORIES

PASSPORT STAMPS

Canaveral
National Seashore

EST. 1975 — 57,661.69 ACRES — 28° 46' 3" N, 80° 46' 37" W

DATE(S) I VISITED:

WHO I WENT WITH:

Sticker

SIGHTS & WILDLIFE

MY FAVORITE MEMORIES

PASSPORT STAMPS

Cane River Creole
National Historical Park

LA

EST. 1994 — 205.5 ACRES — 31° 39' 56" N, 93° 0' 10" W

DATE(S) I VISITED:

WHO I WENT WITH:

Sticker

SIGHTS & WILDLIFE

MY FAVORITE MEMORIES

PASSPORT STAMPS

Cape Hatteras
National Seashore

NC

EST. 1953 — 30,350.65 ACRES — 35° 18' 13" N, 75° 30' 41" W

DATE(S) I VISITED:

Sticker

WHO I WENT WITH:

SIGHTS & WILDLIFE

MY FAVORITE MEMORIES

PASSPORT STAMPS

Cape Lookout
National Seashore

NC

EST. 1966 — 28,243.36 ACRES — 34° 36' 19" N, 76° 32' 11" W

DATE(S) I VISITED:

WHO I WENT WITH:

Sticker

SIGHTS & WILDLIFE

MY FAVORITE MEMORIES

PASSPORT STAMPS

139

Carl Sandburg Home
National Historic Site

 NC

EST. 1968 — 268.49 ACRES — 35° 16' 4" N, 82° 27' 6" W

DATE(S) I VISITED:

Sticker

WHO I WENT WITH:

SIGHTS & WILDLIFE

MY FAVORITE MEMORIES

PASSPORT STAMPS

Castillo de San Marcos
National Monument

FL

EST. 1924 — 19.38 ACRES — 29° 53' 52" N, 81° 18' 41" W

DATE(S) I VISITED:

Sticker

WHO I WENT WITH:

SIGHTS & WILDLIFE

MY FAVORITE MEMORIES

PASSPORT STAMPS

Cedar Creek and Belle Grove
National Historical Park

VA

EST. 2002 — 3,704.96 ACRES — 39° 10' 3" N, 78° 18' 3" W

DATE(S) I VISITED:

Sticker

WHO I WENT WITH:

SIGHTS & WILDLIFE

MY FAVORITE MEMORIES

PASSPORT STAMPS

Charles Pinckney
National Historic Site

EST. 1988 — 28.45 ACRES — 32° 50' 46" N, 79° 49' 29" W

DATE(S) I VISITED:

WHO I WENT WITH:

Sticker

SIGHTS & WILDLIFE

MY FAVORITE MEMORIES

PASSPORT STAMPS

Chattahoochee River
National Recreation Area

EST. 1978 — 12,416.75 ACRES — 33° 59' 14" N, 84° 19' 29" W

DATE(S) I VISITED:

Sticker

WHO I WENT WITH:

SIGHTS & WILDLIFE

MY FAVORITE MEMORIES

PASSPORT STAMPS

Chickamauga & Chattanooga
National Military Park

GA & TN

EST. 1890 — 9,523.48 ACRES — 34° 56' 24" N, 85° 15' 36" W

DATE(S) I VISITED:

WHO I WENT WITH:

Sticker

SIGHTS & WILDLIFE

MY FAVORITE MEMORIES

PASSPORT STAMPS

Christiansted
National Historic Site

EST. 1952 — 27.15 ACRES — 17° 44' 49" N, 64° 42' 8" W

DATE(S) I VISITED:

WHO I WENT WITH:

Sticker

SIGHTS & WILDLIFE

MY FAVORITE MEMORIES

PASSPORT STAMPS

Colonial
National Historical Park

EST. 1930 — 8,675.04 ACRES — 37° 13' 8" N, 76° 31' 3" W

DATE(S) I VISITED:

WHO I WENT WITH:

Sticker

SIGHTS & WILDLIFE

MY FAVORITE MEMORIES

PASSPORT STAMPS

Congaree
National Park

EST. 2003 — 26,693 ACRES — 33° 46' 48" N, 80° 46' 48" W

DATE(S) I VISITED:

WHO I WENT WITH:

Sticker

SIGHTS & WILDLIFE

MY FAVORITE MEMORIES

PASSPORT STAMPS

Cowpens
National Battlefield

SC

EST. 1929 — 841.56 ACRES — 35° 8' 12" N, 81° 49' 5" W

DATE(S) I VISITED:

WHO I WENT WITH:

Sticker

SIGHTS & WILDLIFE

MY FAVORITE MEMORIES

PASSPORT STAMPS

Cumberland Gap
National Historical Park

TN, KY, & VA

EST. 1940 — 24,546.83 ACRES — 36° 36' 15" N, 83° 41' 14" W

DATE(S) I VISITED:

Sticker

WHO I WENT WITH:

SIGHTS & WILDLIFE

MY FAVORITE MEMORIES

PASSPORT STAMPS

Cumberland Island
National Seashore

EST. 1972 — 36,346.83 ACRES — 30° 50' 0" N, 81° 27' 0" W

DATE(S) I VISITED:

WHO I WENT WITH:

Sticker

SIGHTS & WILDLIFE

MY FAVORITE MEMORIES

PASSPORT STAMPS

De Soto
National Memorial

EST. 1948 — 30 ACRES — 27° 31' 26" N, 82° 38' 40" W

DATE(S) I VISITED:

Sticker

WHO I WENT WITH:

SIGHTS & WILDLIFE

MY FAVORITE MEMORIES

PASSPORT STAMPS

Dry Tortugas
National Park

FL

EST. 1992 — 64,701 ACRES — 24° 37' 48" N, 82° 52' 12" W

DATE(S) I VISITED:

WHO I WENT WITH:

Sticker

SIGHTS & WILDLIFE

MY FAVORITE MEMORIES

PASSPORT STAMPS

Everglades
National Park

 FL

EST. 1934 — 1,508,939 ACRES — 25° 19' 12" N, 80° 55' 48" W

DATE(S) I VISITED:

Sticker

WHO I WENT WITH:

SIGHTS & WILDLIFE

MY FAVORITE MEMORIES

PASSPORT STAMPS

Fort Caroline
National Memorial

FL

EST. 1953 — 138.39 ACRES — 30° 23' 13" N, 81° 30' 2" W

DATE(S) I VISITED:

Sticker

WHO I WENT WITH:

SIGHTS & WILDLIFE

MY FAVORITE MEMORIES

PASSPORT STAMPS

Fort Donelson
National Battlefield

EST. 1928 — 1,319.00 ACRES — 36° 29' 14" N, 87° 51' 39" W

DATE(S) I VISITED:

WHO I WENT WITH:

Sticker

SIGHTS & WILDLIFE

MY FAVORITE MEMORIES

PASSPORT STAMPS

KY & TN

Fort Frederica
National Monument

EST. 1936 — 305.34 ACRES — 31° 13' 25.82" N, 81° 23' 35.66" W

GA

DATE(S) I VISITED:

WHO I WENT WITH:

Sticker

SIGHTS & WILDLIFE

MY FAVORITE MEMORIES

PASSPORT STAMPS

Fort Matanzas
National Monument

EST. 1924 — 300.11 ACRES — 29° 42' 55" N, 81° 14' 21" W

FL

DATE(S) I VISITED:

WHO I WENT WITH:

Sticker

SIGHTS & WILDLIFE

MY FAVORITE MEMORIES

PASSPORT STAMPS

Fort Monroe
National Monument

EST. 2011 — 367.12 ACRES — 37° 0' 13" N, 76° 18' 27" W

DATE(S) I VISITED:

Sticker

WHO I WENT WITH:

SIGHTS & WILDLIFE

MY FAVORITE MEMORIES

PASSPORT STAMPS

Fort Pulaski
National Monument

EST. 1924 — 5,623.10 ACRES — 32° 1' 38" N, 80° 53' 25" W

DATE(S) I VISITED:

Sticker

WHO I WENT WITH:

SIGHTS & WILDLIFE

MY FAVORITE MEMORIES

PASSPORT STAMPS

Fort Raleigh
National Historic Site

NC

EST. 1941 — 515.73 ACRES — 35° 56' 19" N, 75° 42' 36" W

DATE(S) I VISITED:

WHO I WENT WITH:

Sticker

SIGHTS & WILDLIFE

MY FAVORITE MEMORIES

PASSPORT STAMPS

Fort Sumter and Fort Moultrie
National Historical Park

SC

EST. 2019 — 232.52 ACRES — 32° 45' 8" N, 79° 52' 29" W

DATE(S) I VISITED:

Sticker

WHO I WENT WITH:

SIGHTS & WILDLIFE

MY FAVORITE MEMORIES

PASSPORT STAMPS

Fredericksburg and Spotsylvania
National Military Park

VA

EST. 1927 — 8,405.46 ACRES — 38° 17' 35" N, 77° 28' 9" W

DATE(S) I VISITED:

Sticker

WHO I WENT WITH:

SIGHTS & WILDLIFE

MY FAVORITE MEMORIES

PASSPORT STAMPS

Freedom Riders
National Monument

EST. 2017 — 7.83 ACRES — 33° 38' 6" N, 85° 54' 30" W

AL

DATE(S) I VISITED:

Sticker

WHO I WENT WITH:

SIGHTS & WILDLIFE

MY FAVORITE MEMORIES

PASSPORT STAMPS

164

Gauley River
National Recreation Area

WV

EST. 1988 — 11,565.75 ACRES — 38° 13' 12" N, 80° 53' 24" W

DATE(S) I VISITED:

WHO I WENT WITH:

Sticker

SIGHTS & WILDLIFE

MY FAVORITE MEMORIES

PASSPORT STAMPS

George Washington Birthplace
National Monument

VA

EST. 1930 — 654.19 ACRES — 38° 11' 8" N, 76° 54' 59" W

DATE(S) I VISITED:

Sticker

WHO I WENT WITH:

SIGHTS & WILDLIFE

MY FAVORITE MEMORIES

PASSPORT STAMPS

Great Smoky Mountains
National Park

TN & NC

EST. 1934 — 522,427 ACRES — 35° 40' 48" N, 83° 31' 48" W

DATE(S) I VISITED:

WHO I WENT WITH:

Sticker

SIGHTS & WILDLIFE

MY FAVORITE MEMORIES

PASSPORT STAMPS

Guilford Courthouse
National Military Park

NC

EST. 1917 — 254.44 ACRES — 36° 7' 53" N, 79° 50' 47" W

DATE(S) I VISITED:

Sticker

WHO I WENT WITH:

SIGHTS & WILDLIFE

MY FAVORITE MEMORIES

PASSPORT STAMPS

Gulf Islands
National Seashore

FL & MS

EST. 1971 — 138,305.52 ACRES — 30° 21' 52" N, 86° 58' 3" W

DATE(S) I VISITED:

Sticker

WHO I WENT WITH:

SIGHTS & WILDLIFE

MY FAVORITE MEMORIES

PASSPORT STAMPS

Harpers Ferry
National Historical Park

WV, VA, & MD

EST. 1944 — 3,669.19 ACRES — 39° 19' 22" N, 77° 43' 47" W

DATE(S) I VISITED:

Sticker

WHO I WENT WITH:

SIGHTS & WILDLIFE

MY FAVORITE MEMORIES

PASSPORT STAMPS

Horseshoe Bend
National Military Park

AL

EST. 1956 — 2,040.00 ACRES — 32° 58' 15" N, 85° 44' 18" W

DATE(S) I VISITED:

WHO I WENT WITH:

Sticker

SIGHTS & WILDLIFE

MY FAVORITE MEMORIES

PASSPORT STAMPS

Jean Lafitte

LA

National Historical Park and Preserve

EST. 1907 — 25,875.86 ACRES — 29° 56' 33" N, 89° 59' 39" W

DATE(S) I VISITED:

Sticker

WHO I WENT WITH:

SIGHTS & WILDLIFE

MY FAVORITE MEMORIES

PASSPORT STAMPS

Jimmy Carter
National Historical Park

 GA

EST. 1987 — 78.35 ACRES — 32° 1' 49.58" N, 84° 25' 5.69" W

DATE(S) I VISITED:

WHO I WENT WITH:

SIGHTS & WILDLIFE

Sticker

MY FAVORITE MEMORIES

PASSPORT STAMPS

Kennesaw Mountain
National Battlefield Park

EST. 1917 — 2,913.63 ACRES — 33° 58' 59" N, 84° 34' 41" W

DATE(S) I VISITED:

Sticker

WHO I WENT WITH:

SIGHTS & WILDLIFE

MY FAVORITE MEMORIES

PASSPORT STAMPS

Kings Mountain
National Military Park

SC

EST. 1933 — 3,945.29 ACRES — 35° 8' 16" N, 81° 23' 22" W

DATE(S) I VISITED:

Sticker

WHO I WENT WITH:

SIGHTS & WILDLIFE

MY FAVORITE MEMORIES

PASSPORT STAMPS

Little River Canyon
National Preserve

EST. 1992 — 15,291.63 ACRES — 34° 26' 26" N, 85° 35' 44" W

DATE(S) I VISITED:

Sticker

WHO I WENT WITH:

SIGHTS & WILDLIFE

MY FAVORITE MEMORIES

PASSPORT STAMPS

Maggie L. Walker
National Historic Site

VA

EST. 1978 — 1.29 ACRES — 37° 32' 52" N, 77° 26' 17" W

DATE(S) I VISITED:

WHO I WENT WITH:

Sticker

SIGHTS & WILDLIFE

MY FAVORITE MEMORIES

PASSPORT STAMPS

Mammoth Cave
National Park

EST. 1941 — 54,016 ACRES — 37° 10' 48" N, 86° 6' 0" W

DATE(S) I VISITED:

Sticker

WHO I WENT WITH:

SIGHTS & WILDLIFE

MY FAVORITE MEMORIES

PASSPORT STAMPS

Manassas
National Battlefield Park

VA

EST. 1936 — 5,073.44 ACRES — 38° 48' 46" N, 77° 31' 18" W

DATE(S) I VISITED:

Sticker

WHO I WENT WITH:

SIGHTS & WILDLIFE

MY FAVORITE MEMORIES

PASSPORT STAMPS

179

Manhattan Project
National Historical Park

TN, NM, & WA

EST. 2015 — 113.61 ACRES — 36° 0' 37.2852" N 84° 16' 10.7256" W

DATE(S) I VISITED:

Sticker

WHO I WENT WITH:

SIGHTS & WILDLIFE

MY FAVORITE MEMORIES

PASSPORT STAMPS

Martin Luther King, Jr.
National Historical Park

EST. 1980 — 39.17 ACRES — 33° 45' 18" N, 84° 22' 20" W

DATE(S) I VISITED:

Sticker

WHO I WENT WITH:

SIGHTS & WILDLIFE

MY FAVORITE MEMORIES

PASSPORT STAMPS

Medgar and Myrlie Evers Home
National Monument

EST. 2020 — 0.74 ACRES — 32° 20' 27.49" N, 90° 12' 45.54" W

DATE(S) I VISITED:

WHO I WENT WITH:

Sticker

SIGHTS & WILDLIFE

MY FAVORITE MEMORIES

PASSPORT STAMPS

Mill Springs Battlefield
National Monument

KY

EST. 2020 — 1,459.19 ACRES — 37° 4' 8" N, 84° 44' 10" W

DATE(S) I VISITED:

WHO I WENT WITH:

Sticker

SIGHTS & WILDLIFE

MY FAVORITE MEMORIES

PASSPORT STAMPS

Moores Creek
National Battlefield

EST. 1926 — 87.75 ACRES — 34° 27' 29.6" N, 78° 6' 37.1" W

NC

Sticker

DATE(S) I VISITED:

WHO I WENT WITH:

SIGHTS & WILDLIFE

MY FAVORITE MEMORIES

PASSPORT STAMPS

Natchez
National Historical Park

EST. 1988 — 119.75 ACRES — 31° 32' 36" N, 91° 22' 59" W

DATE(S) I VISITED:

Sticker

WHO I WENT WITH:

SIGHTS & WILDLIFE

MY FAVORITE MEMORIES

PASSPORT STAMPS

Natchez Trace
Parkway

EST. 1938 — 444 mi ACRES — 35° 59' 11.76" N, 86° 59' 32.28" W

DATE(S) I VISITED:

Sticker

WHO I WENT WITH:

SIGHTS & WILDLIFE

MY FAVORITE MEMORIES

PASSPORT STAMPS

Natchez Trace
National Scenic Trail

MS, AL, & TN

EST. 1983 — 60 Miles ACRES — 34° 40' 3.81" N, 88° 5' 17.93" W

Sticker

DATE(S) I VISITED:

WHO I WENT WITH:

SIGHTS & WILDLIFE

MY FAVORITE MEMORIES

PASSPORT STAMPS

New Orleans Jazz
National Historical Park

LA

EST. 1994 — 5.13 ACRES — 29° 57' 47" N, 90° 4' 5" W

DATE(S) I VISITED:

Sticker

WHO I WENT WITH:

SIGHTS & WILDLIFE

MY FAVORITE MEMORIES

PASSPORT STAMPS

Ninety Six
National Historic Site

EST. 1976 — 1,021.94 ACRES — 34° 8' 49" N, 82° 1' 28" W

SC

DATE(S) I VISITED:

Sticker

WHO I WENT WITH:

SIGHTS & WILDLIFE

MY FAVORITE MEMORIES

PASSPORT STAMPS

New River Gorge
National Park and Preserve

WV

EST. 1919 — 147,243 ACRES — 37° 18' 0" N, 113° 3' 0" W

DATE(S) I VISITED:

Sticker

WHO I WENT WITH:

SIGHTS & WILDLIFE

MY FAVORITE MEMORIES

PASSPORT STAMPS

Obed
Wild and Scenic River

EST. 1976 — 5,489.85 ACRES — 36° 4' 31" N, 84° 38' 58" W

DATE(S) I VISITED:

Sticker

WHO I WENT WITH:

SIGHTS & WILDLIFE

MY FAVORITE MEMORIES

PASSPORT STAMPS

Ocmulgee Mounds
National Historical Park

EST. 1936 — 3,431.05 ACRES — 32° 50' 12" N, 83° 36' 30" W

DATE(S) I VISITED:

Sticker

WHO I WENT WITH:

SIGHTS & WILDLIFE

MY FAVORITE MEMORIES

PASSPORT STAMPS

Petersburg
National Battlefield

EST. 1926 — 9,350.56 ACRES — 37° 13' 10" N, 77° 21' 41" W

DATE(S) I VISITED:

WHO I WENT WITH:

Sticker

SIGHTS & WILDLIFE

MY FAVORITE MEMORIES

PASSPORT STAMPS

Poverty Point
National Monument

EST. 1988 — 910.85 ACRES — 32° 38' 12" N, 91° 24' 41" W

DATE(S) I VISITED:

Sticker

WHO I WENT WITH:

SIGHTS & WILDLIFE

MY FAVORITE MEMORIES

PASSPORT STAMPS

Prince William Forest Park

EST. 1936 — 16,059.91 ACRES — 38° 35' 7" N, 77° 22' 47" W

DATE(S) I VISITED:

WHO I WENT WITH:

Sticker

SIGHTS & WILDLIFE

MY FAVORITE MEMORIES

PASSPORT STAMPS

Reconstruction Era
National Historical Park

 SC

EST. 2017 — 64.99 ACRES — 32° 25' 57" N, 80° 40' 14" W

DATE(S) I VISITED:

Sticker

WHO I WENT WITH:

SIGHTS & WILDLIFE

MY FAVORITE MEMORIES

PASSPORT STAMPS

Richmond
National Battlefield Park

EST. 1936 — 8,143.26 ACRES — 37° 25' 45" N, 77° 22' 25" W

DATE(S) I VISITED:

WHO I WENT WITH:

Sticker

SIGHTS & WILDLIFE

MY FAVORITE MEMORIES

PASSPORT STAMPS

197

Russell Cave
National Monument

EST. 1961 — 310.45 ACRES — 34° 58' 35.83" N, 85° 48' 51.3" W

AL

DATE(S) I VISITED:

WHO I WENT WITH:

Sticker

SIGHTS & WILDLIFE

MY FAVORITE MEMORIES

PASSPORT STAMPS

Salt River Bay National
Historical Park and Ecological Preserve

VI

EST. 1988 — 46,000 ACRES — 30° 27' 16.02" N, 81° 26' 59.57" W

DATE(S) I VISITED:

WHO I WENT WITH:

Sticker

SIGHTS & WILDLIFE

MY FAVORITE MEMORIES

PASSPORT STAMPS

San Juan
National Historic Site

EST. 1949 — 75.13 ACRES — 18° 28' 3" N, 66° 6' 37" W

DATE(S) I VISITED:

WHO I WENT WITH:

Sticker

SIGHTS & WILDLIFE

MY FAVORITE MEMORIES

PASSPORT STAMPS

Shenandoah
National Park

EST. 1890 — 404,063 ACRES — 36° 25' 48" N, 118° 40' 48" W

DATE(S) I VISITED:

WHO I WENT WITH:

Sticker

SIGHTS & WILDLIFE

MY FAVORITE MEMORIES

PASSPORT STAMPS

Shiloh
National Military Park

 TN & MS

EST. 1894 — 9,322.10 ACRES — 35° 8' 12" N, 88° 20' 26" W

DATE(S) I VISITED:

Sticker

WHO I WENT WITH:

SIGHTS & WILDLIFE

MY FAVORITE MEMORIES

PASSPORT STAMPS

Stones River
National Battlefield

EST. 1927 — 709.49 ACRES — 35° 52' 34" N, 86° 25' 51" W

TN

DATE(S) I VISITED:

Sticker

WHO I WENT WITH:

SIGHTS & WILDLIFE

MY FAVORITE MEMORIES

PASSPORT STAMPS

Timucuan
Ecological and Historic Preserve

FL

EST. 1988 — 46,000 ACRES — 30° 27' 16.02" N, 81° 26' 59.57" W

DATE(S) I VISITED:

Sticker

WHO I WENT WITH:

SIGHTS & WILDLIFE

MY FAVORITE MEMORIES

PASSPORT STAMPS

Tupelo
National Battlefield

EST. 1929 — 1 ACRES — 34° 15' 20.4" N, 88° 44' 13.2" W

DATE(S) I VISITED:

WHO I WENT WITH:

Sticker

SIGHTS & WILDLIFE

MY FAVORITE MEMORIES

PASSPORT STAMPS

Tuskegee Airmen
National Historic Site

EST. 1978 — 89.68 ACRES — 38° 31' 52.2" N, 77° 2' 21.3" W

AL

DATE(S) I VISITED:

Sticker

WHO I WENT WITH:

SIGHTS & WILDLIFE

MY FAVORITE MEMORIES

PASSPORT STAMPS

Tuskegee Institute
National Historic Site

EST. 1998 — 57.92 ACRES — 32° 27' 33" N, 85° 40' 48" W

AL

DATE(S) I VISITED:

Sticker

WHO I WENT WITH:

SIGHTS & WILDLIFE

MY FAVORITE MEMORIES

PASSPORT STAMPS

Vicksburg
National Military Park

EST. 1899 — 2,524.11 ACRES — 32° 21' 55" N, 90° 50' 32" W

DATE(S) I VISITED:

Sticker

WHO I WENT WITH:

SIGHTS & WILDLIFE

MY FAVORITE MEMORIES

PASSPORT STAMPS

Virgin Islands
National Park

EST. 1978 — 70,447 ACRES — 46° 58' 12" N, 103° 27' 0" W

DATE(S) I VISITED:

WHO I WENT WITH:

Sticker

SIGHTS & WILDLIFE

MY FAVORITE MEMORIES

PASSPORT STAMPS

Virgin Islands Coral Reef
National Monument

EST. 2001 — 12,708.07 ACRES — 18° 18' 22" N, 64° 43' 37" W

DATE(S) I VISITED:

Sticker

WHO I WENT WITH:

SIGHTS & WILDLIFE

MY FAVORITE MEMORIES

PASSPORT STAMPS

Wolf Trap National Park
for the Performing Arts

VA

EST. 1966 — 130.28 ACRES — 38° 56' 13" N, 77° 15' 43" W

DATE(S) I VISITED:

WHO I WENT WITH:

Sticker

SIGHTS & WILDLIFE

MY FAVORITE MEMORIES

PASSPORT STAMPS

Wright Brothers
National Memorial

NC

EST. 1927 — 428.44 ACRES — 36° 0' 51.48" N, 75° 40' 4.44" W

DATE(S) I VISITED:

Sticker

WHO I WENT WITH:

SIGHTS & WILDLIFE

MY FAVORITE MEMORIES

PASSPORT STAMPS

_____

_____

_____

EST. _____ — _____ ACRES — ___° ___' ___" N, ___° ___' ___" W

DATE(S) I VISITED:

WHO I WENT WITH:

Sticker

SIGHTS & WILDLIFE

MY FAVORITE MEMORIES

PASSPORT STAMPS

EST. _____ — _____ **ACRES** — __° __' __" **N,** __° __' __" **W**

DATE(S) I VISITED:

Sticker

WHO I WENT WITH:

SIGHTS & WILDLIFE

MY FAVORITE MEMORIES

PASSPORT STAMPS

_____

EST. _____ — _____ ACRES — ___° ___' ___" N, ___° ___' ___" W

DATE(S) I VISITED:

WHO I WENT WITH:

Sticker

SIGHTS & WILDLIFE

MY FAVORITE MEMORIES

PASSPORT STAMPS

_____

__

EST. _____ — _____ ACRES — __° __' __" N, __° __' __" W

DATE(S) I VISITED:

Sticker

WHO I WENT WITH:

SIGHTS & WILDLIFE

MY FAVORITE MEMORIES

PASSPORT STAMPS

Midwest

Arkansas ~ Illinois ~ Indiana ~ Iowa ~ Kansas ~ Michigan ~ Minnesota ~ Missouri ~ Nebraska ~ North Dakota ~ Ohio ~ South Dakota ~ Wisconsin

Midwest Units by State

Arkansas
- Arkansas Post NMEM
- Buffalo NR
- Fort Smith NHS[1]
- Hot Springs NP
- Little Rock Central High School NHS
- Pea Ridge NMP
- President William Jefferson Clinton Birthplace Home NHS

Illinois
- Lincoln Home NHS
- Pullman NM

Indiana
- George Rogers Clark NHP
- Indiana Dunes NP
- Lincoln Boyhood NMEM

Iowa
- Effigy Mounds NM
- Herbert Hoover NHS

Kansas
- Brown v. Board of Education NHS
- Fort Larned NHS
- Fort Scott NHS
- Nicodemus NHS
- Tallgrass Prairie NPRES

Michigan
- Isle Royale NP
- Keweenaw NHP
- Pictured Rocks NL
- River Raisin NBP
- Sleeping Bear Dunes NL

Minnesota
- Grand Portage NM
- Mississippi NR & RA
- Pipestone NM
- Saint Croix NSR[2]
- Voyageurs NP

Missouri
- Gateway Arch NP
- George Washington Carver NM
- Harry S Truman NHS
- Ozark NSR
- Ste. Genevieve NHP
- Ulysses S. Grant NHS
- Wilson's Creek NB

Nebraska
- Agate Fossil Beds NM
- Homestead NHP
- Missouri NRR[3]
- Niobrara NSR
- Scotts Bluff NM

North Dakota
- Fort Union Trading Post NHS[4]
- Knife River Indian Villages NHS
- Theodore Roosevelt NP

Ohio
- Charles Young Buffalo Soldiers NM
- Cuyahoga Valley NP
- Dayton Aviation Heritage NHP
- First Ladies NHS
- Hopewell Culture NHP
- James A. Garfield NHS
- Perry's Victory and International Peace Memorial
- William Howard Taft NHS

South Dakota
- Badlands NP
- Jewel Cave NM
- Minuteman Missile NHS
- Mount Rushmore NMEM
- Wind Cave NP

Wisconsin
- Apostle Islands NL

Notes:
1 - Also located in Oklahoma.
2 - Also located in Wisconsin.
3 - Also located in South Dakota.
4 - Also located in Montana.

Agate Fossil Beds
National Monument

NE

EST. 1997 — 3,057.87 ACRES — 42° 25' 18.13" N, 103° 45' 13.97" W

DATE(S) I VISITED:

Sticker

WHO I WENT WITH:

SIGHTS & WILDLIFE

MY FAVORITE MEMORIES

PASSPORT STAMPS

Apostle Islands
National Lakeshore

EST. 1970 — 69,377.43 ACRES — 46° 57' 55" N, 90° 39' 51" W

WI

DATE(S) I VISITED:

Sticker

WHO I WENT WITH:

SIGHTS & WILDLIFE

MY FAVORITE MEMORIES

PASSPORT STAMPS

Arkansas Post
National Memorial

EST. 1960 — 757.51 ACRES — 34° 1' 8.4" N, 91° 20' 56.4" W

AR

Sticker

DATE(S) I VISITED:

WHO I WENT WITH:

SIGHTS & WILDLIFE

MY FAVORITE MEMORIES

PASSPORT STAMPS

221

Badlands
National Park

EST. 1978 — 242,756 ACRES — 43° 45' 0" N, 102° 30' 0" W

SD

DATE(S) I VISITED:

Sticker

WHO I WENT WITH:

SIGHTS & WILDLIFE

MY FAVORITE MEMORIES

PASSPORT STAMPS

Brown v. Board of Education
National Historic Site

EST. 1992 — 1.85 ACRES — 39° 2' 17" N, 95° 40' 35" W

DATE(S) I VISITED:

Sticker

WHO I WENT WITH:

SIGHTS & WILDLIFE

MY FAVORITE MEMORIES

PASSPORT STAMPS

Buffalo
National River

EST. 1992 — 94,293.08 ACRES — 35° 59' 7.8432" N 92° 45' 27.5472" W

DATE(S) I VISITED:

WHO I WENT WITH:

Sticker

SIGHTS & WILDLIFE

MY FAVORITE MEMORIES

PASSPORT STAMPS

Charles Young Buffalo Soldiers
National Monument

OH

EST. 2013 — 59.66 ACRES — 35° 13' 38.28" N, 118° 33' 41.04" W

DATE(S) I VISITED:

WHO I WENT WITH:

Sticker

SIGHTS & WILDLIFE

MY FAVORITE MEMORIES

PASSPORT STAMPS

Cuyahoga Valley
National Park

EST. 2000 — 32,572 ACRES — 41° 14' 24" N, 81° 33' 0" W

DATE(S) I VISITED:

WHO I WENT WITH:

Sticker

SIGHTS & WILDLIFE

MY FAVORITE MEMORIES

PASSPORT STAMPS

Dayton Aviation Heritage
National Historical Park

OH

EST. 1992 — 110.56 ACRES — 39° 47' 41" N, 84° 5' 20" W

DATE(S) I VISITED:

Sticker

WHO I WENT WITH:

SIGHTS & WILDLIFE

MY FAVORITE MEMORIES

PASSPORT STAMPS

Effigy Mounds
National Monument

EST. 1949 — 2,526.39 ACRES — 43° 5' 19.68" N, 91° 11' 8.16" W

IA

DATE(S) I VISITED:

Sticker

WHO I WENT WITH:

SIGHTS & WILDLIFE

MY FAVORITE MEMORIES

PASSPORT STAMPS

First Ladies
National Historic Site

EST. 2000 — 0.46 ACRES — 40° 47' 48" N, 81° 22' 31" W

DATE(S) I VISITED:

WHO I WENT WITH:

Sticker

SIGHTS & WILDLIFE

MY FAVORITE MEMORIES

PASSPORT STAMPS

Fort Larned
National Historic Site

KS

EST. 1964 — 718.39 ACRES — 38° 10' 59" N, 99° 13' 5" W

DATE(S) I VISITED:

Sticker

WHO I WENT WITH:

SIGHTS & WILDLIFE

MY FAVORITE MEMORIES

PASSPORT STAMPS

Fort Scott
National Historic Site

EST. 1978 — 20.11 ACRES — 37° 50' 38" N, 94° 42' 17" W

KS

DATE(S) I VISITED:

Sticker

WHO I WENT WITH:

SIGHTS & WILDLIFE

MY FAVORITE MEMORIES

PASSPORT STAMPS

231

Fort Smith
National Historic Site

AR & OK

EST. 1961 — 75 ACRES — 35° 23' 17.56" N, 94° 25' 47.4" W

DATE(S) I VISITED:

WHO I WENT WITH:

Sticker

SIGHTS & WILDLIFE

MY FAVORITE MEMORIES

PASSPORT STAMPS

Fort Union Trading Post
National Historic Site

ND & MT

EST. 1966 — 440.14 ACRES — 47° 59' 58" N, 104° 2' 26" W

DATE(S) I VISITED:

Sticker

WHO I WENT WITH:

SIGHTS & WILDLIFE

MY FAVORITE MEMORIES

PASSPORT STAMPS

Gateway Arch
National Park

EST. 2018 — 193 ACRES — 38° 37' 48" N, 90° 11' 24" W

DATE(S) I VISITED:

WHO I WENT WITH:

Sticker

SIGHTS & WILDLIFE

MY FAVORITE MEMORIES

PASSPORT STAMPS

George Rogers Clark
National Historical Park

IN

EST. 1966 — 26.17 ACRES — 38° 40' 45.1" N, 87° 32' 8.14" W

DATE(S) I VISITED:

Sticker

WHO I WENT WITH:

SIGHTS & WILDLIFE

MY FAVORITE MEMORIES

PASSPORT STAMPS

George Washington Carver
National Monument

EST. 1943 — 240 ACRES — 36° 59' 10.9" N, 94° 21' 15.09" W

MO

DATE(S) I VISITED:

Sticker

WHO I WENT WITH:

SIGHTS & WILDLIFE

MY FAVORITE MEMORIES

PASSPORT STAMPS

Grand Portage
National Monument

EST. 1960 — 709.97 ACRES — 47° 59' 47" N, 89° 44' 3" W

DATE(S) I VISITED:

Sticker

WHO I WENT WITH:

SIGHTS & WILDLIFE

MY FAVORITE MEMORIES

PASSPORT STAMPS

Harry S Truman
National Historic Site

MO

EST. 1983 — 12.59 ACRES — 39° 5' 36" N, 94° 25' 23" W

DATE(S) I VISITED:

Sticker

WHO I WENT WITH:

SIGHTS & WILDLIFE

MY FAVORITE MEMORIES

PASSPORT STAMPS

Herbert Hoover
National Historic Site

EST. 1965 — 186.8 ACRES — 41° 40' 8" N, 91° 20' 53" W

IA

DATE(S) I VISITED:

WHO I WENT WITH:

Sticker

SIGHTS & WILDLIFE

MY FAVORITE MEMORIES

PASSPORT STAMPS

Homestead
National Historical Park

EST. 1936 — 210.45 ACRES — 40° 17' 7" N, 96° 49' 19" W

DATE(S) I VISITED:

Sticker

WHO I WENT WITH:

SIGHTS & WILDLIFE

MY FAVORITE MEMORIES

PASSPORT STAMPS

Hopewell Culture
National Historical Park

EST. 1923 — 1,775.78 ACRES — 39° 22' 33" N, 83° 0' 23" W

DATE(S) I VISITED:

Sticker

WHO I WENT WITH:

SIGHTS & WILDLIFE

MY FAVORITE MEMORIES

PASSPORT STAMPS

Hot Springs
National Park

AR

EST. 1921 — 5,554 ACRES — 34° 30' 36" N, 93° 3' 0" W

DATE(S) I VISITED:

Sticker

WHO I WENT WITH:

SIGHTS & WILDLIFE

MY FAVORITE MEMORIES

PASSPORT STAMPS

Indiana Dunes
National Park

EST. 2019 — 15,349 ACRES — 41° 39' 11.88" N, 87° 3' 8.64" W

DATE(S) I VISITED:

Sticker

WHO I WENT WITH:

SIGHTS & WILDLIFE

MY FAVORITE MEMORIES

PASSPORT STAMPS

243

Isle Royale
National Park

MI

EST. 1940 — 571,790 ACRES — 48° 6' 0" N, 88° 33' 0" W

DATE(S) I VISITED:

WHO I WENT WITH:

Sticker

SIGHTS & WILDLIFE

MY FAVORITE MEMORIES

PASSPORT STAMPS

James A. Garfield
National Historic Site

EST. 1980 — 7.82 ACRES — 41° 39' 50.26" N, 81° 21' 3.26" W

Sticker

DATE(S) I VISITED:

WHO I WENT WITH:

SIGHTS & WILDLIFE

MY FAVORITE MEMORIES

PASSPORT STAMPS

Jewel Cave
National Monument

SD

EST. 1908 — 1,273.51 ACRES — 43° 43' 46" N, 103° 49' 46" W

DATE(S) I VISITED:

Sticker

WHO I WENT WITH:

SIGHTS & WILDLIFE

MY FAVORITE MEMORIES

PASSPORT STAMPS

Keweenaw
National Historical Park

EST. 1992 — 1,870.00 ACRES — 47° 9' 23" N, 88° 33' 49" W

MI

DATE(S) I VISITED:

WHO I WENT WITH:

Sticker

SIGHTS & WILDLIFE

MY FAVORITE MEMORIES

PASSPORT STAMPS

Knife River Indian Villages
National Historic Site

EST. 1974 — 1,751.00 ACRES — 47° 21' 15" N, 101° 23' 9" W

DATE(S) I VISITED:

Sticker

WHO I WENT WITH:

SIGHTS & WILDLIFE

MY FAVORITE MEMORIES

PASSPORT STAMPS

Lincoln Boyhood
National Memorial

EST. 1962 — 199.96 ACRES — 38° 7' 6" N, 86° 59' 49" W

DATE(S) I VISITED:

Sticker

WHO I WENT WITH:

SIGHTS & WILDLIFE

MY FAVORITE MEMORIES

PASSPORT STAMPS

Lincoln Home
National Historic Site

EST. 1971 — 12.24 ACRES — 39° 47' 50" N, 89° 38' 42" W

DATE(S) I VISITED:

Sticker

WHO I WENT WITH:

SIGHTS & WILDLIFE

MY FAVORITE MEMORIES

PASSPORT STAMPS

Little Rock Central High School
National Historic Site

EST. 1998 — 28.22 ACRES — 34° 44' 12.48" N, 92° 17' 56.04" W

AR

DATE(S) I VISITED:

Sticker

WHO I WENT WITH:

SIGHTS & WILDLIFE

MY FAVORITE MEMORIES

PASSPORT STAMPS

Minuteman Missile
National Historic Site

EST. 1999 — 43.8 ACRES — 43° 55' 52" N, 102° 9' 38" W

DATE(S) I VISITED:

Sticker

WHO I WENT WITH:

SIGHTS & WILDLIFE

MY FAVORITE MEMORIES

PASSPORT STAMPS

Mississippi
National River and Recreation Area

MN

EST. 1978 — 48,456.55 ACRES — 42° 51' 45" N, 97° 23' 34" W

DATE(S) I VISITED:

Sticker

WHO I WENT WITH:

SIGHTS & WILDLIFE

MY FAVORITE MEMORIES

PASSPORT STAMPS

Missouri
National Recreational River

EST. 1988 — 53,775.00 ACRES — 44° 52' 23.88" N, 93° 1' 7.78" W

DATE(S) I VISITED:

Sticker

WHO I WENT WITH:

SIGHTS & WILDLIFE

MY FAVORITE MEMORIES

PASSPORT STAMPS

Mount Rushmore
National Memorial

EST. 1925 — 1,278.45 ACRES — 43° 52' 44" N, 103° 27' 35" W

DATE(S) I VISITED:

Sticker

WHO I WENT WITH:

SIGHTS & WILDLIFE

MY FAVORITE MEMORIES

PASSPORT STAMPS

255

Nicodemus
National Historic Site

KS

EST. 1996 — 4.39 ACRES — 39° 23' 27" N, 99° 37' 3" W

DATE(S) I VISITED:

Sticker

WHO I WENT WITH:

SIGHTS & WILDLIFE

MY FAVORITE MEMORIES

PASSPORT STAMPS

Niobrara
National Scenic River

EST. 1991 — 29,088.57 ACRES — 42° 53' 0" N, 100° 19' 0" W

NE

Sticker

DATE(S) I VISITED:

WHO I WENT WITH:

SIGHTS & WILDLIFE

MY FAVORITE MEMORIES

PASSPORT STAMPS

Ozark
National Scenic Riverways

EST. 1964 — 80,784.30 ACRES — 37° 11' 26.52" N, 91° 16' 34.68" W

DATE(S) I VISITED:

Sticker

WHO I WENT WITH:

SIGHTS & WILDLIFE

MY FAVORITE MEMORIES

PASSPORT STAMPS

Pea Ridge
National Military Park

EST. (1956) — 4,300.35 ACRES — 36° 27' 15" N, 94° 2' 4.9" W

AR

DATE(S) I VISITED:

WHO I WENT WITH:

Sticker

SIGHTS & WILDLIFE

MY FAVORITE MEMORIES

PASSPORT STAMPS

Perry's Victory and International Peace Memorial

OH

EST. 1936 — 25.38 ACRES — 41° 39' 15" N, 82° 48' 41" W

DATE(S) I VISITED:

Sticker

WHO I WENT WITH:

SIGHTS & WILDLIFE

MY FAVORITE MEMORIES

PASSPORT STAMPS

Pictured Rocks
National Lakeshore

EST. 1966 — 73,235.97 ACRES — 46° 33' 44" N, 86° 18' 45" W

MI

DATE(S) I VISITED:

Sticker

WHO I WENT WITH:

SIGHTS & WILDLIFE

MY FAVORITE MEMORIES

PASSPORT STAMPS

Pipestone
National Monument

EST. 1937 — 281.78 ACRES — 36° 51' 43" N, 112° 44' 14" W

DATE(S) I VISITED:

Sticker

WHO I WENT WITH:

SIGHTS & WILDLIFE

MY FAVORITE MEMORIES

PASSPORT STAMPS

President William Jefferson Clinton Birthplace Home
National Historic Site

AR

EST. 2010 — 0.68 ACRES — 33° 40' 1.82" N, 93° 35' 47.36" W

DATE(S) I VISITED:

Sticker

WHO I WENT WITH:

SIGHTS & WILDLIFE

MY FAVORITE MEMORIES

PASSPORT STAMPS

Pullman
National Monument

EST. (2015) — 203.48 ACRES — 41° 41' 50" N, 87° 36' 34" W

IL

Sticker

DATE(S) I VISITED:

WHO I WENT WITH:

SIGHTS & WILDLIFE

MY FAVORITE MEMORIES

PASSPORT STAMPS

River Raisin
National Battlefield Park

EST. 2009 — 42.18 ACRES — 41° 54' 49" N, 83° 22' 42" W

MI

DATE(S) I VISITED:

WHO I WENT WITH:

Sticker

SIGHTS & WILDLIFE

MY FAVORITE MEMORIES

PASSPORT STAMPS

Saint Croix
National Scenic Riverway

MN & WI

EST. 1968 — 67,466.63 ACRES — 45° 23' 21" N, 92° 39' 27" W

DATE(S) I VISITED:

WHO I WENT WITH:

Sticker

SIGHTS & WILDLIFE

MY FAVORITE MEMORIES

PASSPORT STAMPS

Scotts Bluff
National Monument

NE

EST. 1919 — 3,004.73 ACRES — 41° 50' 5" N, 103° 42' 26" W

DATE(S) I VISITED:

Sticker

WHO I WENT WITH:

SIGHTS & WILDLIFE

MY FAVORITE MEMORIES

PASSPORT STAMPS

Sleeping Bear Dunes
National Lakeshore

MI

EST. 1970 — 71,310.35 ACRES — 44° 51' 0" N, 86° 3' 0" W

DATE(S) I VISITED:

WHO I WENT WITH:

Sticker

SIGHTS & WILDLIFE

MY FAVORITE MEMORIES

PASSPORT STAMPS

Ste. Genevieve
National Historical Park

EST. 2020 — 16.91 ACRES — 37° 58' 37.06" N, 90° 2' 55.22" W

MO

DATE(S) I VISITED:

WHO I WENT WITH:

Sticker

SIGHTS & WILDLIFE

MY FAVORITE MEMORIES

PASSPORT STAMPS

Tallgrass Prairie
National Preserve

KS

EST. 1996 — 10,882.67 ACRES — 38° 25' 58" N, 96° 33' 32" W

DATE(S) I VISITED:

Sticker

WHO I WENT WITH:

SIGHTS & WILDLIFE

MY FAVORITE MEMORIES

PASSPORT STAMPS

Theodore Roosevelt
National Park

EST. 1935 — 200,192 ACRES — 38° 31' 48" N, 78° 21' 0" W

DATE(S) I VISITED:

WHO I WENT WITH:

Sticker

SIGHTS & WILDLIFE

MY FAVORITE MEMORIES

PASSPORT STAMPS

Ulysses S. Grant
National Historic Site

MO

EST. 1989 — 9.6 ACRES — 38° 33' 4" N, 90° 21' 7" W

DATE(S) I VISITED:

Sticker

WHO I WENT WITH:

SIGHTS & WILDLIFE

MY FAVORITE MEMORIES

PASSPORT STAMPS

Voyageurs
National Park

EST. 1956 — 15,052 ACRES — 18° 19' 48" N, 64° 43' 48" W

DATE(S) I VISITED:

WHO I WENT WITH:

Sticker

SIGHTS & WILDLIFE

MY FAVORITE MEMORIES

PASSPORT STAMPS

William Howard Taft
National Historic Site

OH

EST. 1969 — 3.64 ACRES — 39° 7' 11" N, 84° 30' 31" W

DATE(S) I VISITED:

Sticker

WHO I WENT WITH:

SIGHTS & WILDLIFE

MY FAVORITE MEMORIES

PASSPORT STAMPS

Wilson's Creek
National Battlefield

EST. 1960 — 2,421.76 ACRES — 37° 6' 56" N, 93° 25' 12" W

MO

DATE(S) I VISITED:

Sticker

WHO I WENT WITH:

SIGHTS & WILDLIFE

MY FAVORITE MEMORIES

PASSPORT STAMPS

275

Wind Cave
National Park

EST. 2019 — 146,344 ACRES — 32° 46' 48" N, 106° 10' 12" W

DATE(S) I VISITED:

Sticker

WHO I WENT WITH:

SIGHTS & WILDLIFE

MY FAVORITE MEMORIES

PASSPORT STAMPS

_____

EST. _____ — _____ ACRES — __° __' __" N, __° __' __" W

DATE(S) I VISITED:

WHO I WENT WITH:

Sticker

SIGHTS & WILDLIFE

MY FAVORITE MEMORIES

PASSPORT STAMPS

_____

_____

—

EST. _____ — _____ ACRES — ___° ___' ___" N, ___° ___' ___" W

DATE(S) I VISITED:

Sticker

WHO I WENT WITH:

SIGHTS & WILDLIFE

MY FAVORITE MEMORIES

PASSPORT STAMPS

EST. _____ — _____ ACRES — ___° ___' ___" N, ___° ___' ___" W

DATE(S) I VISITED:

WHO I WENT WITH:

Sticker

SIGHTS & WILDLIFE

MY FAVORITE MEMORIES

PASSPORT STAMPS

EST. _____ — _____ ACRES — __° __' __" N, __° __' __" W

DATE(S) I VISITED:

Sticker

WHO I WENT WITH:

SIGHTS & WILDLIFE

MY FAVORITE MEMORIES

PASSPORT STAMPS

Southwest

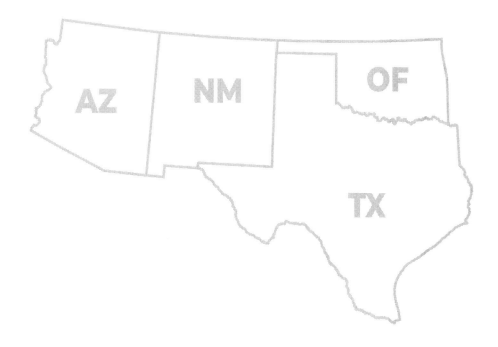

Arizona ~ New Mexico ~ Oklahoma ~ Texas

Southwest Units by State

Arizona[1] [2]

- Canyon De Chelly NM
- Casa Grande Ruins NM
- Chiricahua NM
- Coronado NMEM
- Fort Bowie NHS
- Grand Canyon NP
- Hohokam Pima NM
- Hubbell Trading Post NHS
- Montezuma Castle NM
- Navajo NM
- Organ Pipe Cactus NM
- Petrified Forest NP
- Pipe Spring NM
- Saguaro NP
- Sunset Crater Volcano NM
- Tonto NM
- Tumacacori NHP
- Tuzigoot NM
- Walnut Canyon NM
- Wupatki NM

New Mexico[3]

- Aztec Ruins NM
- Bandelier NM
- Capulin Volcano NM
- Carlsbad Caverns NP
- Chaco Culture NHP
- El Malpais NM
- El Morro NM
- Fort Union NM
- Gila Cliff Dwellings NM
- Pecos NHP
- Petroglyph NM
- Salinas Pueblo Missions NM
- Valles Caldera NPRES
- White Sands NP

Oklahoma[4]

- Chickasaw NRA
- Washita Battlefield NHS

Texas

- Alibates Flint Quarries NM
- Amistad NRA
- Big Bend NP
- Big Thicket NPRES
- Chamizal NMEM
- Fort Davis NHS
- Guadalupe Mountains NP
- Lake Meredith NRA
- Lyndon B. Johnson NHP
- Padre Island NS
- Palo Alto Battlefield NHP
- Rio Grande WSR
- San Antonio Missions NHP
- Waco Mammoth NM

Notes:

1 - Glen Canyon NRA can be found in the Rockies Region under Utah.

2 - Lake Mead NRA can be found in the West Region under Nevada.

3 - Manhattan Project NHP can be found in the Southeast Region under Tennessee.

4 - Fort Smith NHS can be found in the Midwest Region under Arkansas.

Alibates Flint Quarries
National Monument

EST. 1965 — 1,371 ACRES — 35° 34' 30.16" N, 101° 41' 1.63" W

DATE(S) I VISITED:

WHO I WENT WITH:

Sticker

SIGHTS & WILDLIFE

MY FAVORITE MEMORIES

PASSPORT STAMPS

Amistad
National Recreation Area

EST. 1965 — 62,945.15 ACRES — 29° 26' 12" N, 101° 3' 0" W

TX

DATE(S) I VISITED:

WHO I WENT WITH:

Sticker

SIGHTS & WILDLIFE

MY FAVORITE MEMORIES

PASSPORT STAMPS

Aztec Ruins
National Monument

EST. 1923 — 318 ACRES — 36° 50' 9.01" N, 107° 59' 53.24" W

NM

DATE(S) I VISITED:

WHO I WENT WITH:

Sticker

SIGHTS & WILDLIFE

MY FAVORITE MEMORIES

PASSPORT STAMPS

Bandelier
National Monument

EST. 1916 — 33,677 ACRES — 35° 46' 44" N, 106° 19' 16" W

DATE(S) I VISITED:

Sticker

WHO I WENT WITH:

SIGHTS & WILDLIFE

MY FAVORITE MEMORIES

PASSPORT STAMPS

Big Bend
National Park

EST. 1944 — 801,163 ACRES — 29° 15' 0" N, 103° 15' 0" W

DATE(S) I VISITED:

WHO I WENT WITH:

Sticker

SIGHTS & WILDLIFE

MY FAVORITE MEMORIES

PASSPORT STAMPS

Big Thicket
National Preserve

EST. 1974 — 113,121.96 ACRES — 30° 32' 48" N, 94° 20' 25" W

DATE(S) I VISITED:

WHO I WENT WITH:

Sticker

SIGHTS & WILDLIFE

MY FAVORITE MEMORIES

PASSPORT STAMPS

Canyon De Chelly
National Monument

EST. 1931 — 83,840.00 ACRES — 36° 9' 19.01" N, 109° 30' 32.38" W

AZ

DATE(S) I VISITED:

Sticker

WHO I WENT WITH:

SIGHTS & WILDLIFE

MY FAVORITE MEMORIES

PASSPORT STAMPS

Capulin Volcano
National Monument

NM

EST. 1916 — 792.84 ACRES — 67° 20' 0" N, 163° 35' 0" W

DATE(S) I VISITED:

WHO I WENT WITH:

Sticker

SIGHTS & WILDLIFE

MY FAVORITE MEMORIES

PASSPORT STAMPS

Carlsbad Caverns
National Park

NM

EST. 1930 — 46,766 ACRES — 32° 10' 12" N, 104° 26' 24" W

DATE(S) I VISITED:

WHO I WENT WITH:

Sticker

SIGHTS & WILDLIFE

MY FAVORITE MEMORIES

PASSPORT STAMPS

Casa Grande Ruins
National Monument

AZ

EST. 1918 — 472.5 ACRES — 67° 20' 0" N, 163° 35' 0" W

DATE(S) I VISITED:

Sticker

WHO I WENT WITH:

SIGHTS & WILDLIFE

MY FAVORITE MEMORIES

PASSPORT STAMPS

Chaco Culture
National Historical Park

EST. 1907 — 33,960.19 ACRES — 36° 3' 36" N, 107° 57' 36" W

DATE(S) I VISITED:

WHO I WENT WITH:

Sticker

SIGHTS & WILDLIFE

MY FAVORITE MEMORIES

PASSPORT STAMPS

NM

TX

Chamizal
National Memorial

EST. 1974 — 54.9 ACRES — 31° 46' 4" N, 106° 27' 15" W

DATE(S) I VISITED:

Sticker

WHO I WENT WITH:

SIGHTS & WILDLIFE

MY FAVORITE MEMORIES

PASSPORT STAMPS

Chickasaw
National Recreation Area

EST. 1902 — 9,898.63 ACRES — 34° 30' 2" N, 96° 58' 20" W

OK

DATE(S) I VISITED:

Sticker

WHO I WENT WITH:

SIGHTS & WILDLIFE

MY FAVORITE MEMORIES

PASSPORT STAMPS

Chiricahua
National Monument

EST. 1924 — 12024.73 ACRES — 35° 13' 38.28" N, 118° 33' 41.04" W

DATE(S) I VISITED:

WHO I WENT WITH:

Sticker

SIGHTS & WILDLIFE

MY FAVORITE MEMORIES

PASSPORT STAMPS

Coronado
National Memorial

EST. 1952 — 4,830.22 ACRES — 31° 20' 54" N, 110° 16' 18" W

AZ

DATE(S) I VISITED:

Sticker

WHO I WENT WITH:

SIGHTS & WILDLIFE

MY FAVORITE MEMORIES

PASSPORT STAMPS

El Malpais
National Monument

EST. 1987 — 114,347.12 ACRES — 34° 52' 38" N, 108° 3' 3" W

NM

Sticker

DATE(S) I VISITED:

WHO I WENT WITH:

SIGHTS & WILDLIFE

MY FAVORITE MEMORIES

PASSPORT STAMPS

El Morro
National Monument

EST. 1906 — 1,278.72 ACRES — 35° 2' 18" N, 108° 21' 12" W

NM

DATE(S) I VISITED:

WHO I WENT WITH:

Sticker

SIGHTS & WILDLIFE

MY FAVORITE MEMORIES

PASSPORT STAMPS

Fort Bowie
National Historic Site

AZ

EST. 1972 — 999.45 ACRES — 32° 8' 46" N, 109° 26' 8" W

DATE(S) I VISITED:

WHO I WENT WITH:

Sticker

SIGHTS & WILDLIFE

MY FAVORITE MEMORIES

PASSPORT STAMPS

Fort Davis
National Historic Site

EST. 1961 — 523 ACRES — 30° 35' 57" N, 103° 53' 34" W

DATE(S) I VISITED:

Sticker

WHO I WENT WITH:

SIGHTS & WILDLIFE

MY FAVORITE MEMORIES

PASSPORT STAMPS

Fort Union
National Monument

EST. 1954 — 720.6 ACRES — 35° 54' 25.2" N, 105° 0' 54" W

NM

DATE(S) I VISITED:

Sticker

WHO I WENT WITH:

SIGHTS & WILDLIFE

MY FAVORITE MEMORIES

PASSPORT STAMPS

Gila Cliff Dwellings
National Monument

NM

EST. 1907 — 533.13 ACRES — 33° 13' 38" N, 108° 16' 20" W

DATE(S) I VISITED:

Sticker

WHO I WENT WITH:

SIGHTS & WILDLIFE

MY FAVORITE MEMORIES

PASSPORT STAMPS

Grand Canyon
National Park

AZ

EST. 1919 — 1,201,647 ACRES — 36° 3' 36" N, 112° 8' 24" W

DATE(S) I VISITED:

Sticker

WHO I WENT WITH:

SIGHTS & WILDLIFE

MY FAVORITE MEMORIES

PASSPORT STAMPS

Guadalupe Mountains
National Park

EST. 1966 — 86,367 ACRES — 31° 55' 12" N, 104° 52' 12" W

DATE(S) I VISITED:

WHO I WENT WITH:

Sticker

SIGHTS & WILDLIFE

MY FAVORITE MEMORIES

PASSPORT STAMPS

Hohokam Pima
National Monument

 AZ

EST. 1972 — 1,690.00 ACRES — 33° 11' 15" N, 111° 55' 28.2" W

DATE(S) I VISITED:

Sticker

WHO I WENT WITH:

SIGHTS & WILDLIFE

MY FAVORITE MEMORIES

PASSPORT STAMPS

Hubbell Trading Post
National Historic Site

EST. 1967 — 160.09 ACRES — 35° 43' 26" N, 109° 33' 36" W

DATE(S) I VISITED:

WHO I WENT WITH:

Sticker

SIGHTS & WILDLIFE

MY FAVORITE MEMORIES

PASSPORT STAMPS

Lake Meredith
National Recreation Area

TX

EST. 1990 — 44,977.63 ACRES — 35° 42' 53" N, 101° 33' 10" W

DATE(S) I VISITED:

Sticker

WHO I WENT WITH:

SIGHTS & WILDLIFE

MY FAVORITE MEMORIES

PASSPORT STAMPS

Lyndon B. Johnson
National Historical Park

EST. 1969 — 1,571.71 ACRES — 30° 14' 27" N, 98° 37' 27" W

DATE(S) I VISITED:

WHO I WENT WITH:

Sticker

SIGHTS & WILDLIFE

MY FAVORITE MEMORIES

PASSPORT STAMPS

Montezuma Castle
National Monument

EST. 1906 — 1,015.52 ACRES — 34° 36' 40" N, 111° 50' 12" W

DATE(S) I VISITED:

Sticker

WHO I WENT WITH:

SIGHTS & WILDLIFE

MY FAVORITE MEMORIES

PASSPORT STAMPS

Navajo
National Monument

EST. 1909 — 360 ACRES — 36° 40' 41.99" N, 110° 32' 27.5" W

DATE(S) I VISITED:

Sticker

WHO I WENT WITH:

SIGHTS & WILDLIFE

MY FAVORITE MEMORIES

PASSPORT STAMPS

Organ Pipe Cactus
National Monument

AZ

EST. 1937 — 330,688.86 ACRES — 31° 57' 14.4" N, 112° 48' 3.6" W

DATE(S) I VISITED:

Sticker

WHO I WENT WITH:

SIGHTS & WILDLIFE

MY FAVORITE MEMORIES

PASSPORT STAMPS

Padre Island
National Seashore

EST. 1962 — 130,434.27 ACRES — 26° 59' 4" N, 97° 22' 50" W

TX

DATE(S) I VISITED:

Sticker

WHO I WENT WITH:

SIGHTS & WILDLIFE

MY FAVORITE MEMORIES

PASSPORT STAMPS

Palo Alto Battlefield
National Historical Park

TX

EST. 1915 — 3,426.87 ACRES — 26° 1' 17" N, 97° 28' 50" W

DATE(S) I VISITED:

Sticker

WHO I WENT WITH:

SIGHTS & WILDLIFE

MY FAVORITE MEMORIES

PASSPORT STAMPS

Pecos
National Historical Park

EST. 1965 — 6,693.49 ACRES — 35° 33' 0" N, 105° 41' 4" W

NM

DATE(S) I VISITED:

WHO I WENT WITH:

Sticker

SIGHTS & WILDLIFE

MY FAVORITE MEMORIES

PASSPORT STAMPS

Petrified Forest
National Park

EST. 1938 — 922,649 ACRES — 47° 58' 12" N, 123° 30' 0" W

DATE(S) I VISITED:

Sticker

WHO I WENT WITH:

SIGHTS & WILDLIFE

MY FAVORITE MEMORIES

PASSPORT STAMPS

Petroglyph
National Monument

NM

EST. 1990 — 7,209.04 ACRES — 35° 8' 9" N, 106° 45' 43" W

DATE(S) I VISITED:

Sticker

WHO I WENT WITH:

SIGHTS & WILDLIFE

MY FAVORITE MEMORIES

PASSPORT STAMPS

Pipe Spring
National Monument

EST. 1923 — 40.00 ACRES — 36° 51' 43" N, 112° 44' 14" W

DATE(S) I VISITED:

WHO I WENT WITH:

Sticker

SIGHTS & WILDLIFE

MY FAVORITE MEMORIES

PASSPORT STAMPS

Rio Grande
Wild and Scenic River

EST. 1968 — 13,123.39 ACRES — 29° 29' 0" N, 103° 18' 0" W

DATE(S) I VISITED:

Sticker

WHO I WENT WITH:

SIGHTS & WILDLIFE

MY FAVORITE MEMORIES

PASSPORT STAMPS

Saguaro
National Park

EST. 1915 — 265,807 ACRES — 40° 24' 0" N, 105° 34' 48" W

AZ

Sticker

DATE(S) I VISITED:

WHO I WENT WITH:

SIGHTS & WILDLIFE

MY FAVORITE MEMORIES

PASSPORT STAMPS

Salinas Pueblo Missions
National Monument

NM

EST. 1909 — 1,071.42 ACRES — 34° 15' 35" N, 106° 5' 25" W

DATE(S) I VISITED:

Sticker

WHO I WENT WITH:

SIGHTS & WILDLIFE

MY FAVORITE MEMORIES

PASSPORT STAMPS

San Antonio Missions
National Historical Park

TX

EST. 1983 — 990.28 ACRES — 29° 21' 42" N, 98° 28' 49" W

DATE(S) I VISITED:

Sticker

WHO I WENT WITH:

SIGHTS & WILDLIFE

MY FAVORITE MEMORIES

PASSPORT STAMPS

Sunset Crater Volcano
National Monument

AZ

EST. 1930 — 3,040.00 ACRES — 35° 21' 52" N, 111° 30' 13" W

DATE(S) I VISITED:

WHO I WENT WITH:

Sticker

SIGHTS & WILDLIFE

MY FAVORITE MEMORIES

PASSPORT STAMPS

Tonto
National Monument

EST. 1907 — 1,120.00 ACRES — 33° 39' 25" N, 111° 5' 40" W

DATE(S) I VISITED:

Sticker

WHO I WENT WITH:

SIGHTS & WILDLIFE

MY FAVORITE MEMORIES

PASSPORT STAMPS

Tumacacori
National Historical Park

EST. 1990 — 360.32 ACRES — 31° 34' 5.33" N, 111° 3' 2.33" W

AZ

DATE(S) I VISITED:

WHO I WENT WITH:

Sticker

SIGHTS & WILDLIFE

MY FAVORITE MEMORIES

PASSPORT STAMPS

Tuzigoot
National Monument

EST. 1939 — 811.89 ACRES — 34° 46' 15.07" N, 112° 1' 33.57" W

AZ

DATE(S) I VISITED:

Sticker

WHO I WENT WITH:

SIGHTS & WILDLIFE

MY FAVORITE MEMORIES

PASSPORT STAMPS

Valles Caldera
National Preserve

EST. 2000 — 89,766.09 ACRES — 35° 54' 0" N, 106° 31' 58.8" W

NM

DATE(S) I VISITED:

Sticker

WHO I WENT WITH:

SIGHTS & WILDLIFE

MY FAVORITE MEMORIES

PASSPORT STAMPS

Waco Mammoth
National Monument

TX

EST. 2015 — 107.23 ACRES — 31° 36' 21.6" N, 97° 10' 30" W

DATE(S) I VISITED:

WHO I WENT WITH:

Sticker

SIGHTS & WILDLIFE

MY FAVORITE MEMORIES

PASSPORT STAMPS

Walnut Canyon
National Monument

AZ

EST. 2015 — 3,200.60 ACRES — 35° 9' 57" N, 111° 30' 7" W

DATE(S) I VISITED:

WHO I WENT WITH:

Sticker

SIGHTS & WILDLIFE

MY FAVORITE MEMORIES

PASSPORT STAMPS

Washita Battlefield
National Historic Site

OK

EST. 1996 — 315.2 ACRES — 35° 37' 3" N, 99° 42' 1" W

DATE(S) I VISITED:

Sticker

WHO I WENT WITH:

SIGHTS & WILDLIFE

MY FAVORITE MEMORIES

PASSPORT STAMPS

White Sands
National Park

NM

EST. 1975 — 218,222 ACRES — 48° 30' 0" N, 92° 52' 48" W

DATE(S) I VISITED:

Sticker

WHO I WENT WITH:

SIGHTS & WILDLIFE

MY FAVORITE MEMORIES

PASSPORT STAMPS

Wupatki
National Monument

AZ

EST. 1924 — 35,401.83 ACRES — 35° 33' 27" N, 111° 23' 45" W

DATE(S) I VISITED:

Sticker

WHO I WENT WITH:

SIGHTS & WILDLIFE

MY FAVORITE MEMORIES

PASSPORT STAMPS

EST. _____ — _____ ACRES — __° __' __" N, __° __' __" W

DATE(S) I VISITED:

Sticker

WHO I WENT WITH:

SIGHTS & WILDLIFE

MY FAVORITE MEMORIES

PASSPORT STAMPS

_____

_____

___ EST. _____ — _____ ACRES — ___° ___' ___" N, ___° ___' ___" W

DATE(S) I VISITED:

WHO I WENT WITH:

Sticker

SIGHTS & WILDLIFE

MY FAVORITE MEMORIES

PASSPORT STAMPS

_____

_____

—   EST. _____ — _____ ACRES — ___° ___' ___" N, ___° ___' ___" W

DATE(S) I VISITED:

WHO I WENT WITH:

Sticker

SIGHTS & WILDLIFE

MY FAVORITE MEMORIES

PASSPORT STAMPS

——

EST. _____ — _____ ACRES — ___° ___' ___" N, ___° ___' ___" W

DATE(S) I VISITED:

WHO I WENT WITH:

Sticker

SIGHTS & WILDLIFE

MY FAVORITE MEMORIES

PASSPORT STAMPS

Rockies

Colorado ~ Montana ~ Utah ~ Wyoming

Rockies Units by State

Colorado
- Bent's Old Fort NHS
- Black Canyon of the Gunnison NP
- Colorado NM
- Curecanti NRA
- Dinosaur NM[1]
- Florissant Fossil Beds NM
- Great Sand Dunes NP & PRES
- Hovenweep NM[1]
- Mesa Verde NP
- Rocky Mountain NP
- Sand Creek Massacre NHS
- Yucca House NM

Montana[2]
- Big Hole NB
- Bighorn Canyon NRA
- Glacier NP
- Grant-Kohrs Ranch NHS
- Little Bighorn Battlefield NM

Utah
- Arches NP
- Bryce Canyon NP
- Canyonlands NP
- Capitol Reef NP
- Cedar Breaks NM
- Glen Canyon NRA[3]
- Golden Spike NHP
- Natural Bridges NM
- Rainbow Bridge NM
- Timpanogos Cave NM
- Zion NP

Wyoming
- Devils Tower NM
- Fort Laramie NHS
- Fossil Butte NM
- Grand Teton NP
- John D. Rockefeller Jr. Parkway
- Yellowstone NP[4]

Notes:
1 - Also located in Utah.

2 - Fort Smith NHS can be found in the Midwest Region.

3 - Also located in Arizona.

4 - Also located in Idaho and Montana.

Arches
National Park

EST. 1971 — 76,679 ACRES — 38° 40' 48" N, 109° 34' 12" W

UT

DATE(S) I VISITED:

Sticker

WHO I WENT WITH:

SIGHTS & WILDLIFE

MY FAVORITE MEMORIES

PASSPORT STAMPS

Bent's Old Fort
National Historic Site

CO

EST. 1960 — 798.54 ACRES — 38° 2' 25" N, 103° 25' 47" W

DATE(S) I VISITED:

WHO I WENT WITH:

Sticker

SIGHTS & WILDLIFE

MY FAVORITE MEMORIES

PASSPORT STAMPS

Big Hole
National Battlefield

EST. 1910 — 975.61 ACRES — 45° 38' 15" N, 113° 38' 37" W

MT

DATE(S) I VISITED:

Sticker

WHO I WENT WITH:

SIGHTS & WILDLIFE

MY FAVORITE MEMORIES

PASSPORT STAMPS

Bighorn Canyon
National Recreation Area

MT & WY

EST. 1966 — 120,296.22 ACRES — 45° 11' 40" N, 108° 7' 50" W

DATE(S) I VISITED:

WHO I WENT WITH:

Sticker

SIGHTS & WILDLIFE

MY FAVORITE MEMORIES

PASSPORT STAMPS

Black Canyon of the Gunnison
National Park

CO

EST. 1999 — 30,780 ACRES — 38° 34' 12" N, 107° 43' 12" W

DATE(S) I VISITED:

Sticker

WHO I WENT WITH:

SIGHTS & WILDLIFE

MY FAVORITE MEMORIES

PASSPORT STAMPS

Bryce Canyon
National Park

EST. 1928 — 35,835 ACRES — 37° 34' 12" N, 112° 10' 48" W

UT

DATE(S) I VISITED:

Sticker

WHO I WENT WITH:

SIGHTS & WILDLIFE

MY FAVORITE MEMORIES

PASSPORT STAMPS

Canyonlands
National Park

EST. 1964 — 337,598 ACRES — 38° 12' 0" N, 109° 55' 48" W

UT

Sticker

DATE(S) I VISITED:

WHO I WENT WITH:

SIGHTS & WILDLIFE

MY FAVORITE MEMORIES

PASSPORT STAMPS

Capitol Reef
National Park

EST. 1971 — 241,904 ACRES — 38° 12' 0" N, 111° 10' 12" W

UT

DATE(S) I VISITED:

Sticker

WHO I WENT WITH:

SIGHTS & WILDLIFE

MY FAVORITE MEMORIES

PASSPORT STAMPS

Cedar Breaks
National Monument

UT

EST. 1933 — 6154.6 ACRES — 37° 38' 32.92" N, 112° 50' 55.79" W

DATE(S) I VISITED:

Sticker

WHO I WENT WITH:

SIGHTS & WILDLIFE

MY FAVORITE MEMORIES

PASSPORT STAMPS

Colorado
National Monument

EST. 1911 — 20536.39 ACRES — 39° 2' 33" N, 108° 41' 10" W

CO

DATE(S) I VISITED:

WHO I WENT WITH:

Sticker

SIGHTS & WILDLIFE

MY FAVORITE MEMORIES

PASSPORT STAMPS

Curecanti
National Recreation Area

EST. 1965 — 43,590.56 ACRES — 38° 27' 17" N, 107° 19' 37" W

CO

DATE(S) I VISITED:

WHO I WENT WITH:

Sticker

SIGHTS & WILDLIFE

MY FAVORITE MEMORIES

PASSPORT STAMPS

Devils Tower
National Monument

EST. 1906 — 1,347.21 ACRES — 44° 35' 26" N, 104° 42' 55" W

WY

DATE(S) I VISITED:

Sticker

WHO I WENT WITH:

SIGHTS & WILDLIFE

MY FAVORITE MEMORIES

PASSPORT STAMPS

Dinosaur
National Monument

CO & UT

EST. 1915 — 210,281.92 ACRES — 40° 32' 0" N, 108° 59' 0" W

Sticker

DATE(S) I VISITED:

WHO I WENT WITH:

SIGHTS & WILDLIFE

MY FAVORITE MEMORIES

PASSPORT STAMPS

Florissant Fossil Beds
National Monument

CO

EST. 1969 — 6,278.09 ACRES — 38° 54' 50.4" N, 105° 17' 13.2" W

DATE(S) I VISITED:

Sticker

WHO I WENT WITH:

SIGHTS & WILDLIFE

MY FAVORITE MEMORIES

PASSPORT STAMPS

Fort Laramie
National Historic Site

WY

EST. 1931 — 873.11 ACRES — 42° 12' 33" N, 104° 32' 9.1" W

DATE(S) I VISITED:

WHO I WENT WITH:

Sticker

SIGHTS & WILDLIFE

MY FAVORITE MEMORIES

PASSPORT STAMPS

Fossil Butte
National Monument

WY

EST. 1972 — 8,198.00 ACRES — 41° 51' 52" N, 110° 46' 33" W

DATE(S) I VISITED:

Sticker

WHO I WENT WITH:

SIGHTS & WILDLIFE

MY FAVORITE MEMORIES

PASSPORT STAMPS

Glacier
National Park

EST. 1980 — 3,223,383 ACRES — 58° 30' 0" N, 137° 0' 0" W

MT

DATE(S) I VISITED:

Sticker

WHO I WENT WITH:

SIGHTS & WILDLIFE

MY FAVORITE MEMORIES

PASSPORT STAMPS

Glen Canyon
National Recreation Area

UT & AZ

EST. 1972 — 1,254,116.62 ACRES — 36° 59' 37" N, 111° 29' 13" W

DATE(S) I VISITED:

Sticker

WHO I WENT WITH:

SIGHTS & WILDLIFE

MY FAVORITE MEMORIES

PASSPORT STAMPS

Golden Spike
National Historical Park

EST. 1957 — 2,735.28 ACRES — 41° 37' 4.44" N, 112° 33' 5.76" W

UT

DATE(S) I VISITED:

Sticker

WHO I WENT WITH:

SIGHTS & WILDLIFE

MY FAVORITE MEMORIES

PASSPORT STAMPS

Grand Teton
National Park

EST. 1929 — 310,044 ACRES — 43° 43' 48" N, 110° 48' 0" W

WY

Sticker

DATE(S) I VISITED:

WHO I WENT WITH:

SIGHTS & WILDLIFE

MY FAVORITE MEMORIES

PASSPORT STAMPS

Grant-Kohrs Ranch
National Historic Site

EST. 1972 — 1,618.43 ACRES — 46° 24' 30" N, 112° 44' 22" W

MT

DATE(S) I VISITED:

WHO I WENT WITH:

Sticker

SIGHTS & WILDLIFE

MY FAVORITE MEMORIES

PASSPORT STAMPS

Great Sand Dunes
National Park and Preserve

CO

EST. 2004 — 107,346 ACRES — 37° 43' 48" N, 105° 30' 36" W

DATE(S) I VISITED:

Sticker

WHO I WENT WITH:

SIGHTS & WILDLIFE

MY FAVORITE MEMORIES

PASSPORT STAMPS

Hovenweep
National Monument

EST. 1923 — 784.93 ACRES — 37° 23' 2" N, 109° 4' 38" W

DATE(S) I VISITED:

WHO I WENT WITH:

Sticker

SIGHTS & WILDLIFE

MY FAVORITE MEMORIES

PASSPORT STAMPS

John D. Rockefeller Jr.
Parkway

WY

EST. 1972 — 24,000 ACRES — 44° 6' 17" N, 110° 41' 34" W

DATE(S) I VISITED:

Sticker

WHO I WENT WITH:

SIGHTS & WILDLIFE

MY FAVORITE MEMORIES

PASSPORT STAMPS

Little Bighorn Battlefield
National Monument

MT

EST. 1879 — 765.34 ACRES — 45° 34' 13" N, 107° 25' 39" W

DATE(S) I VISITED:

WHO I WENT WITH:

Sticker

SIGHTS & WILDLIFE

MY FAVORITE MEMORIES

PASSPORT STAMPS

Mesa Verde
National Park

EST. 1906 — 52,485 ACRES — 37° 10' 48" N, 108° 29' 24" W

CO

Sticker

DATE(S) I VISITED:

WHO I WENT WITH:

SIGHTS & WILDLIFE

MY FAVORITE MEMORIES

PASSPORT STAMPS

Natural Bridges
National Monument

EST. 1908 — 7,636.49 ACRES — 37° 36' 4.98" N, 110° 0' 49.48" W

UT

DATE(S) I VISITED:

Sticker

WHO I WENT WITH:

SIGHTS & WILDLIFE

MY FAVORITE MEMORIES

PASSPORT STAMPS

Rainbow Bridge
National Monument

UT

EST. 1910 — 160 ACRES — 37° 4' 38" N, 110° 57' 51" W

DATE(S) I VISITED:

WHO I WENT WITH:

Sticker

SIGHTS & WILDLIFE

MY FAVORITE MEMORIES

PASSPORT STAMPS

Rocky Mountain
National Park

EST. 1968 — 138,999 ACRES — 41° 18' 0" N, 124° 0' 0" W

CO

DATE(S) I VISITED:

WHO I WENT WITH:

Sticker

SIGHTS & WILDLIFE

MY FAVORITE MEMORIES

PASSPORT STAMPS

Sand Creek Massacre
National Historic Site

EST. 2007 — 12,583.34 ACRES — 38° 32' 27" N, 102° 31' 43" W

DATE(S) I VISITED:

WHO I WENT WITH:

Sticker

SIGHTS & WILDLIFE

MY FAVORITE MEMORIES

PASSPORT STAMPS

Timpanogos Cave
National Monument

UT

EST. 1922 — 250 ACRES — 40° 26' 26" N, 111° 42' 34" W

DATE(S) I VISITED:

Sticker

WHO I WENT WITH:

SIGHTS & WILDLIFE

MY FAVORITE MEMORIES

PASSPORT STAMPS

Yellowstone
National Park

WY, ID, & MT

EST. 1980 — 8,323,146 ACRES — 61° 0' 0" N, 142° 0' 0" W

DATE(S) I VISITED:

Sticker

WHO I WENT WITH:

SIGHTS & WILDLIFE

MY FAVORITE MEMORIES

PASSPORT STAMPS

Yucca House
National Monument

EST. 1919 — 33.87 ACRES — 37° 15' 1" N, 108° 41' 11" W

CO

DATE(S) I VISITED:

WHO I WENT WITH:

Sticker

SIGHTS & WILDLIFE

MY FAVORITE MEMORIES

PASSPORT STAMPS

Zion
National Park

UT

EST. 1890 — 761,748 ACRES — 37° 49' 48" N, 119° 30' 0" W

DATE(S) I VISITED:

WHO I WENT WITH:

Sticker

SIGHTS & WILDLIFE

MY FAVORITE MEMORIES

PASSPORT STAMPS

_____

_____

___

EST. _____ — _____ ACRES — __° __' __" N, __° __' __" W

DATE(S) I VISITED:

Sticker

WHO I WENT WITH:

SIGHTS & WILDLIFE

MY FAVORITE MEMORIES

PASSPORT STAMPS

EST. _____ — _____ ACRES — ___° ___' ___" N, ___° ___' ___" W

DATE(S) I VISITED:

Sticker

WHO I WENT WITH:

SIGHTS & WILDLIFE

MY FAVORITE MEMORIES

PASSPORT STAMPS

_____

_____

_____

EST. _____ — _____ ACRES — ___° ___' ___" N, ___° ___' ___" W

DATE(S) I VISITED:

WHO I WENT WITH:

Sticker

SIGHTS & WILDLIFE

MY FAVORITE MEMORIES

PASSPORT STAMPS

_____

_____

EST. _____ — _____ ACRES — ___° ___' ___" N, ___° ___' ___" W

DATE(S) I VISITED:

WHO I WENT WITH:

Sticker

SIGHTS & WILDLIFE

MY FAVORITE MEMORIES

PASSPORT STAMPS

West

American Samoa ~ California ~ Guam ~ Hawaii ~ Nevada

West Units by State

American Samoa
- National Park of American Samoa

California
- Cabrillo NM
- Castle Mountains NM
- César E. Chávez NM
- Channel Islands NP
- Death Valley NP[1]
- Devils Postpile NM
- Eugene O'Neill NHS
- Fort Point NHS
- Golden Gate NRA
- John Muir NHS
- Joshua Tree NP
- Kings Canyon NP
- Lassen Volcanic NP
- Lava Beds NM
- Manzanar NHS
- Mojave NPRES
- Muir Woods NM
- Pinnacles NP
- Point Reyes NS
- Port Chicago Naval Magazine NMEM
- Redwood NP
- Rosie the Riveter World War II Home Front NHP
- San Francisco Maritime NHP
- Santa Monica Mountains NRA
- Sequoia NP
- Tule Lake NM
- Whiskeytown-Shasta-Trinity NRA
- Yosemite NP

Guam
- War in the Pacific NHP

Hawaii
- Haleakala NP
- Hawaii Volcanoes NP
- Honouliuli NHS
- Kalaupapa NHP
- Kaloko-Honokohau NHP
- Pearl Harbor NMEM
- Pu'uhonua O Honaunau NHP
- Pu'ukohola Heiau NHS

Nevada
- Great Basin NP
- Lake Mead NRA[2]
- Tule Springs Fossil Beds NM

Notes:
1 - Also located in Nevada.

2 - Also located in Arizona.

National Park of American Samoa

AS

EST. 1988 — 8,257 ACRES — 14° 15' 0" S, 170° 40' 48" W

DATE(S) I VISITED:

WHO I WENT WITH:

Sticker

SIGHTS & WILDLIFE

MY FAVORITE MEMORIES

PASSPORT STAMPS

Cabrillo
National Monument

EST. 1913 — 159.94 ACRES — 32° 40' 23" N, 117° 14' 19" W

DATE(S) I VISITED:

WHO I WENT WITH:

Sticker

SIGHTS & WILDLIFE

MY FAVORITE MEMORIES

PASSPORT STAMPS

Castle Mountains
National Monument

EST. 2016 — 21025.5 ACRES — 35° 15' 0" N, 115° 6' 36" W

DATE(S) I VISITED:

WHO I WENT WITH:

Sticker

SIGHTS & WILDLIFE

MY FAVORITE MEMORIES

PASSPORT STAMPS

César E. Chávez
National Monument

CA

EST. 2012 — 116.56 ACRES — 35° 13' 38.28" N, 118° 33' 41.04" W

Sticker

DATE(S) I VISITED:

WHO I WENT WITH:

SIGHTS & WILDLIFE

MY FAVORITE MEMORIES

PASSPORT STAMPS

Channel Islands
National Park

EST. 1980 — 249,561 ACRES — 34° 0' 36" N, 119° 25' 12" W

CA

DATE(S) I VISITED:

WHO I WENT WITH:

Sticker

SIGHTS & WILDLIFE

MY FAVORITE MEMORIES

PASSPORT STAMPS

Death Valley
National Park

CA & NV

EST. 1994 — 3,408,396 ACRES — 36° 14' 24" N, 116° 49' 12" W

DATE(S) I VISITED:

Sticker

WHO I WENT WITH:

SIGHTS & WILDLIFE

MY FAVORITE MEMORIES

PASSPORT STAMPS

Devils Postpile
National Monument

EST. 1911 — 800.19 ACRES — 37° 37' 28" N, 119° 5' 4" W

DATE(S) I VISITED:

Sticker

WHO I WENT WITH:

SIGHTS & WILDLIFE

MY FAVORITE MEMORIES

PASSPORT STAMPS

Eugene O'Neill
National Historic Site

CA

EST. 1976 — 13.19 ACRES — 37° 49' 28" N, 122° 1' 47" W

DATE(S) I VISITED:

WHO I WENT WITH:

Sticker

SIGHTS & WILDLIFE

MY FAVORITE MEMORIES

PASSPORT STAMPS

Fort Point
National Historic Site

EST. 1970 — 29 ACRES — 37° 48' 38" N, 122° 28' 38" W

CA

DATE(S) I VISITED:

WHO I WENT WITH:

Sticker

SIGHTS & WILDLIFE

MY FAVORITE MEMORIES

PASSPORT STAMPS

Golden Gate
National Recreation Area

CA

EST. 1972 — 82,116 ACRES — 37° 47' 0" N, 122° 28' 0" W

DATE(S) I VISITED:

WHO I WENT WITH:

Sticker

SIGHTS & WILDLIFE

MY FAVORITE MEMORIES

PASSPORT STAMPS

Great Basin
National Park

EST. 1986 — 77,180 ACRES — 38° 58' 48" N, 114° 18' 0" W

DATE(S) I VISITED:

WHO I WENT WITH:

Sticker

SIGHTS & WILDLIFE

MY FAVORITE MEMORIES

PASSPORT STAMPS

Haleakala
National Park

EST. 1961 — 33,265 ACRES — 20° 43' 12" N, 156° 10' 12" W

HI

Sticker

DATE(S) I VISITED:

WHO I WENT WITH:

SIGHTS & WILDLIFE

MY FAVORITE MEMORIES

PASSPORT STAMPS

Hawai'i Volcanoes
National Park

EST. 1916 — 325,605 ACRES — 19° 22' 48" N, 155° 12' 0" W

DATE(S) I VISITED:

WHO I WENT WITH:

Sticker

SIGHTS & WILDLIFE

MY FAVORITE MEMORIES

PASSPORT STAMPS

Honouliuli
National Historic Site

EST. 2015 — 154.46 ACRES — 21° 23' 30" N, 158° 3' 35" W

HI

DATE(S) I VISITED:

Sticker

WHO I WENT WITH:

SIGHTS & WILDLIFE

MY FAVORITE MEMORIES

PASSPORT STAMPS

John Muir
National Historic Site

EST. 1964 — 344.14 ACRES — 37° 59' 28.72" N, 122° 7' 59.87" W

DATE(S) I VISITED:

Sticker

WHO I WENT WITH:

SIGHTS & WILDLIFE

MY FAVORITE MEMORIES

PASSPORT STAMPS

Joshua Tree
National Park

EST. 1994 — 795,156 ACRES — 33° 47' 24" N, 115° 54' 0" W

Sticker

DATE(S) I VISITED:

WHO I WENT WITH:

SIGHTS & WILDLIFE

MY FAVORITE MEMORIES

PASSPORT STAMPS

Kalaupapa
National Historical Park

EST. 1980 — 10,778.88 ACRES — 21° 10' 40" N, 156° 57' 36" W

HI

DATE(S) I VISITED:

Sticker

WHO I WENT WITH:

SIGHTS & WILDLIFE

MY FAVORITE MEMORIES

PASSPORT STAMPS

Kaloko-Honokohau
National Historical Park

HI

EST. 1978 — 1,163.05 ACRES — 19° 40' 43.32" N, 156° 1' 19.2" W

DATE(S) I VISITED:

Sticker

WHO I WENT WITH:

SIGHTS & WILDLIFE

MY FAVORITE MEMORIES

PASSPORT STAMPS

Kings Canyon
National Park

CA

EST. 1940 — 461,901 ACRES — 36° 48' 0" N, 118° 33' 0" W

DATE(S) I VISITED:

Sticker

WHO I WENT WITH:

SIGHTS & WILDLIFE

MY FAVORITE MEMORIES

PASSPORT STAMPS

Lake Mead
National Recreation Area

NV & AZ

EST. 1936 — 1,495,815.53 ACRES — 48° 19' 19" N, 120° 40' 42" W

DATE(S) I VISITED:

WHO I WENT WITH:

Sticker

SIGHTS & WILDLIFE

MY FAVORITE MEMORIES

PASSPORT STAMPS

Lassen Volcanic
National Park

CA

EST. 1916 — 106,589 ACRES — 40° 29' 24" N, 121° 30' 36" W

DATE(S) I VISITED:

Sticker

WHO I WENT WITH:

SIGHTS & WILDLIFE

MY FAVORITE MEMORIES

PASSPORT STAMPS

Lava Beds
National Monument

CA

EST. 1925 — 46,692.42 ACRES — 41° 42' 50" N, 121° 30' 30" W

DATE(S) I VISITED:

Sticker

WHO I WENT WITH:

SIGHTS & WILDLIFE

MY FAVORITE MEMORIES

PASSPORT STAMPS

Manzanar
National Historic Site

EST. 1992 — 813.81 ACRES — 36° 43' 42" N, 118° 9' 16" W

DATE(S) I VISITED:

WHO I WENT WITH:

Sticker

SIGHTS & WILDLIFE

MY FAVORITE MEMORIES

PASSPORT STAMPS

Mojave
National Preserve

CA

EST. 1994 — 1,549,709.37 ACRES — 34° 53' 0" N, 115° 43' 0" W

DATE(S) I VISITED:

Sticker

WHO I WENT WITH:

SIGHTS & WILDLIFE

MY FAVORITE MEMORIES

PASSPORT STAMPS

Muir Woods
National Monument

EST. 1908 — 553.55 ACRES — 37° 53' 31" N, 122° 34' 15" W

DATE(S) I VISITED:

WHO I WENT WITH:

Sticker

SIGHTS & WILDLIFE

MY FAVORITE MEMORIES

PASSPORT STAMPS

Pearl Harbor
National Memorial

EST. 2019 — 21.64 ACRES — 21° 20' 23.5824" N 157° 58' 15.2436" W

HI

Sticker

DATE(S) I VISITED:

WHO I WENT WITH:

SIGHTS & WILDLIFE

MY FAVORITE MEMORIES

PASSPORT STAMPS

Pinnacles
National Park

EST. 1962 — 221,390 ACRES — 35° 4' 12" N, 109° 46' 48" W

DATE(S) I VISITED:

Sticker

WHO I WENT WITH:

SIGHTS & WILDLIFE

MY FAVORITE MEMORIES

PASSPORT STAMPS

Point Reyes
National Seashore

CA

EST. 1962 — 71,053.38 ACRES — 38° 4' 0" N, 122° 53' 0" W

DATE(S) I VISITED:

WHO I WENT WITH:

SIGHTS & WILDLIFE

Sticker

MY FAVORITE MEMORIES

PASSPORT STAMPS

Port Chicago Naval Magazine
National Memorial

CA

EST. 1992 — 5 ACRES — 38° 3' 27" N, 122° 1' 47" W

DATE(S) I VISITED:

Sticker

WHO I WENT WITH:

SIGHTS & WILDLIFE

MY FAVORITE MEMORIES

PASSPORT STAMPS

Pu'uhonua O Honaunau
National Historical Park

HI

EST. 1955 — 419.8 ACRES — 19° 25' 19" N, 155° 54' 37" W

DATE(S) I VISITED:

Sticker

WHO I WENT WITH:

SIGHTS & WILDLIFE

MY FAVORITE MEMORIES

PASSPORT STAMPS

Pu'ukohola Heiau
National Historic Site

HI

EST. 1972 — 86.24 ACRES — 20° 1' 36" N, 155° 49' 12" W

DATE(S) I VISITED:

Sticker

WHO I WENT WITH:

SIGHTS & WILDLIFE

MY FAVORITE MEMORIES

PASSPORT STAMPS

Redwood
National Park

EST. 2013 — 26,686 ACRES — 36° 28' 48" N, 121° 9' 36" W

DATE(S) I VISITED:

WHO I WENT WITH:

Sticker

SIGHTS & WILDLIFE

MY FAVORITE MEMORIES

PASSPORT STAMPS

Rosie the Riveter World War II Home
Front National Historical Park

EST. 2000 — 145.19 ACRES — 37° 54' 34.36" N, 122° 21' 26.48" W

DATE(S) I VISITED:

Sticker

WHO I WENT WITH:

SIGHTS & WILDLIFE

MY FAVORITE MEMORIES

PASSPORT STAMPS

San Francisco Maritime
National Historical Park

 CA

EST. 1988 — 49.86 ACRES — 37° 48' 23" N, 122° 25' 25" W

DATE(S) I VISITED:

Sticker

WHO I WENT WITH:

SIGHTS & WILDLIFE

MY FAVORITE MEMORIES

PASSPORT STAMPS

Santa Monica Mountains
National Recreation Area

EST. 1978 — 157,698.12 ACRES — 34° 6' 14" N, 118° 36' 9" W

DATE(S) I VISITED:

Sticker

WHO I WENT WITH:

SIGHTS & WILDLIFE

MY FAVORITE MEMORIES

PASSPORT STAMPS

Sequoia
National Park

EST. 1994 — 92,867 ACRES — 32° 15' 0" N, 110° 30' 0" W

DATE(S) I VISITED:

WHO I WENT WITH:

Sticker

SIGHTS & WILDLIFE

MY FAVORITE MEMORIES

PASSPORT STAMPS

Tule Lake
National Monument

CA

EST. 2019 — 37.39 ACRES — 41° 53' 22" N, 121° 22' 29" W

DATE(S) I VISITED:

Sticker

WHO I WENT WITH:

SIGHTS & WILDLIFE

MY FAVORITE MEMORIES

PASSPORT STAMPS

Tule Springs Fossil Beds
National Monument

EST. 2014 — 22,650.00 ACRES — 36° 22' 15.6" N, 115° 18' 21.6" W

DATE(S) I VISITED:

Sticker

WHO I WENT WITH:

SIGHTS & WILDLIFE

MY FAVORITE MEMORIES

PASSPORT STAMPS

War in the Pacific
National Historical Park

EST. 1978 — 2,030.65 ACRES — 13° 25' 21.03" N, 144° 40' 32.38" E

DATE(S) I VISITED:

WHO I WENT WITH:

Sticker

SIGHTS & WILDLIFE

MY FAVORITE MEMORIES

PASSPORT STAMPS

Whiskeytown-Shasta-Trinity
National Recreation Area

CA

EST. 1965 — 42,503.25 ACRES — 40° 37' 31" N, 122° 33' 34" W

DATE(S) I VISITED:

WHO I WENT WITH:

Sticker

SIGHTS & WILDLIFE

MY FAVORITE MEMORIES

PASSPORT STAMPS

Yosemite
National Park

EST. 1872 — 2,219,791 ACRES — 44° 36' 0" N, 110° 30' 0" W

DATE(S) I VISITED:

Sticker

WHO I WENT WITH:

SIGHTS & WILDLIFE

MY FAVORITE MEMORIES

PASSPORT STAMPS

_

EST. _____ — _____ ACRES — __° __' __" N, __° __' __" W

DATE(S) I VISITED:

WHO I WENT WITH:

Sticker

SIGHTS & WILDLIFE

MY FAVORITE MEMORIES

PASSPORT STAMPS

_____

_____

— EST. _____ — _____ ACRES — ___° ___' ___" N, ___° ___' ___" W

DATE(S) I VISITED:

Sticker

WHO I WENT WITH:

SIGHTS & WILDLIFE

MY FAVORITE MEMORIES

PASSPORT STAMPS

_____

_____

EST. _____ — _____ ACRES — ___° ___' ___" N, ___° ___' ___" W

DATE(S) I VISITED:

WHO I WENT WITH:

Sticker

SIGHTS & WILDLIFE

MY FAVORITE MEMORIES

PASSPORT STAMPS

EST. _____ — _____ ACRES — __° __' __" N, __° __' __" W

DATE(S) I VISITED:

WHO I WENT WITH:

Sticker

SIGHTS & WILDLIFE

MY FAVORITE MEMORIES

PASSPORT STAMPS

Pacific NW

Alaska ~ Idaho ~ Oregon ~ Washington

Pacific NW Units by State

Alaska

- Alagnak WR
- Aniakchak NM & NPRES
- Bering Land Bridge NPRES
- Cape Krusenstern NM
- Denali NP & PRES
- Gates of the Arctic NP & PRES
- Glacier Bay NP & PRES
- Katmai NP & PRES
- Kenai Fjords NP
- Klondike Gold Rush NHP[1]
- Kobuk Valley NP
- Lake Clark NP & PRES
- Noatak NPRES
- Sitka NHP
- Wrangell-St. Elias NP & PRES
- Yukon-Charley Rivers NPRES

Idaho[2]

- City of Rocks NRES
- Craters of the Moon MN & PRES
- Hagerman Fossil Beds NM
- Minidoka NHS
- Nez Perce NHP[3]

Oregon

- Crater Lake NP
- John Day Fossil Beds NM
- Lewis and Clark NHP[1]
- Oregon Caves MN & PRES

Washington[4]

- Ebey's Landing NHR
- Fort Vancouver NHS[5]
- Lake Chelan NRA
- Lake Roosevelt NRA
- Mount Rainier NP
- North Cascades NP
- Olympic NP
- Ross Lake NRA
- San Juan Island NHP
- Whitman Mission NHS

Notes:

1 - Also located in Washington.

2 - Yellowstone NP can be found in the Rockies Region.

3 - Also located in Montana, Oregon, and Washington.

4 - Manhattan Project NHP can be found in the Southeast Region under Tennessee

5 - Also located in Oregon.

Alagnak
Wild River

DATE(S) I VISITED:

WHO I WENT WITH:

Sticker

SIGHTS & WILDLIFE

MY FAVORITE MEMORIES

PASSPORT STAMPS

Aniakchak
National Monument and Preserve

EST. 1978 — 601,294 ACRES — 56° 50' 0" N, 158° 15' 0" W

AK

DATE(S) I VISITED:

Sticker

WHO I WENT WITH:

SIGHTS & WILDLIFE

MY FAVORITE MEMORIES

PASSPORT STAMPS

Bering Land Bridge
National Preserve

EST. 1978 — 2,697,391.01 ACRES — 65° 50' 0" N, 164° 10' 0" W

DATE(S) I VISITED:

Sticker

WHO I WENT WITH:

SIGHTS & WILDLIFE

MY FAVORITE MEMORIES

PASSPORT STAMPS

Cape Krusenstern
National Monument

AK

EST. 1980 — 649,096.15 ACRES — 67° 20' 0" N, 163° 35' 0" W

DATE(S) I VISITED:

WHO I WENT WITH:

Sticker

SIGHTS & WILDLIFE

MY FAVORITE MEMORIES

PASSPORT STAMPS

City of Rocks
National Reserve

EST. 1988 — 14,407.19 ACRES — 42° 4' 11.58" N, 113° 42' 44.68" W

DATE(S) I VISITED:

Sticker

WHO I WENT WITH:

SIGHTS & WILDLIFE

MY FAVORITE MEMORIES

PASSPORT STAMPS

Crater Lake
National Park

EST. 1902 — 183,224 ACRES — 42° 56' 24" N, 122° 6' 0" W

OR

Sticker

DATE(S) I VISITED:

WHO I WENT WITH:

SIGHTS & WILDLIFE

MY FAVORITE MEMORIES

PASSPORT STAMPS

Craters of the Moon
National Monument and Preserve

ID

EST. 1924 — 53437.64 ACRES — 39° 2' 33" N, 108° 41' 10" W

DATE(S) I VISITED:

Sticker

WHO I WENT WITH:

SIGHTS & WILDLIFE

MY FAVORITE MEMORIES

PASSPORT STAMPS

Denali
National Park and Preserve

EST. 1917 — 4,740,911 ACRES — 63° 19' 48" N, 150° 30' 0" W

DATE(S) I VISITED:

Sticker

WHO I WENT WITH:

SIGHTS & WILDLIFE

MY FAVORITE MEMORIES

PASSPORT STAMPS

Ebey's Landing
National Historical Reserve

EST. 1978 — 19,333.51 ACRES — 48° 13' 6" N, 122° 41' 1" W

DATE(S) I VISITED:

Sticker

WHO I WENT WITH:

SIGHTS & WILDLIFE

MY FAVORITE MEMORIES

PASSPORT STAMPS

Fort Vancouver
National Historic Site

EST. 1948 — 206.72 ACRES — 45° 37' 31.42" N, 122° 39' 29.35" W

DATE(S) I VISITED:

Sticker

WHO I WENT WITH:

SIGHTS & WILDLIFE

MY FAVORITE MEMORIES

PASSPORT STAMPS

Gates of the Arctic
National Park and Preserve

AK

EST. 1980 — 7,523,897 ACRES — 67° 46' 48" N, 153° 18' 0" W

DATE(S) I VISITED:

Sticker

WHO I WENT WITH:

SIGHTS & WILDLIFE

MY FAVORITE MEMORIES

PASSPORT STAMPS

Glacier Bay
National Park and Preserve

EST. 1910 — 1,013,126 ACRES — 48° 48' 0" N, 114° 0' 0" W

DATE(S) I VISITED:

WHO I WENT WITH:

Sticker

SIGHTS & WILDLIFE

MY FAVORITE MEMORIES

PASSPORT STAMPS

Hagerman Fossil Beds
National Monument

ID

EST. 1988 — 4,351.15 ACRES — 42° 47' 25" N, 114° 56' 43" W

DATE(S) I VISITED:

WHO I WENT WITH:

Sticker

SIGHTS & WILDLIFE

MY FAVORITE MEMORIES

PASSPORT STAMPS

John Day Fossil Beds
National Monument

EST. 1975 — 14,062.19 ACRES — 44° 33' 21" N, 119° 38' 43" W

DATE(S) I VISITED:

WHO I WENT WITH:

Sticker

SIGHTS & WILDLIFE

MY FAVORITE MEMORIES

PASSPORT STAMPS

Katmai
National Park and Preserve

EST. 1980 — 3,674,529 ACRES — 58° 30' 0" N, 155° 0' 0" W

DATE(S) I VISITED:

WHO I WENT WITH:

Sticker

SIGHTS & WILDLIFE

MY FAVORITE MEMORIES

PASSPORT STAMPS

AK

Kenai Fjords
National Park

EST. 1980 — 669,650 ACRES — 59° 55' 12" N, 149° 39' 0" W

DATE(S) I VISITED:

Sticker

WHO I WENT WITH:

SIGHTS & WILDLIFE

MY FAVORITE MEMORIES

PASSPORT STAMPS

Klondike Gold Rush
National Historical Park

AK & WA

EST. 1976 — 12,996.49 ACRES — 59° 34' 31.33" N, 135° 15' 49.21" W

DATE(S) I VISITED:

WHO I WENT WITH:

Sticker

SIGHTS & WILDLIFE

MY FAVORITE MEMORIES

PASSPORT STAMPS

Kobuk Valley
National Park

EST. 1980 — 1,750,716 ACRES — 67° 33' 0" N, 159° 16' 48" W

DATE(S) I VISITED:

Sticker

WHO I WENT WITH:

SIGHTS & WILDLIFE

MY FAVORITE MEMORIES

PASSPORT STAMPS

Lake Chelan
National Recreation Area

EST. 1968 — 61,939.12 ACRES — 48° 19' 19" N, 120° 40' 42" W

DATE(S) I VISITED:

Sticker

WHO I WENT WITH:

SIGHTS & WILDLIFE

MY FAVORITE MEMORIES

PASSPORT STAMPS

Lake Clark
National Park and Preserve

EST. 1980 — 2,619,816 ACRES — 60° 58' 12" N, 153° 25' 12" W

DATE(S) I VISITED:

Sticker

WHO I WENT WITH:

SIGHTS & WILDLIFE

MY FAVORITE MEMORIES

PASSPORT STAMPS

Lake Roosevelt
National Recreation Area

WA

EST. 1946 — 100,390.31 ACRES — 48° 6' 26.75" N, 118° 12' 46.4" W

DATE(S) I VISITED:

Sticker

WHO I WENT WITH:

SIGHTS & WILDLIFE

MY FAVORITE MEMORIES

PASSPORT STAMPS

Lewis and Clark
National Historical Park

OR & WA

EST. 1958 — 3,410.15 ACRES — 46° 8' 1" N, 123° 52' 39" W

DATE(S) I VISITED:

Sticker

WHO I WENT WITH:

SIGHTS & WILDLIFE

MY FAVORITE MEMORIES

PASSPORT STAMPS

Minidoka
National Historic Site

EST. 2001 — 396.3 ACRES — 42° 40' 44.4" N, 114° 14' 38.4" W

DATE(S) I VISITED:

Sticker

WHO I WENT WITH:

SIGHTS & WILDLIFE

MY FAVORITE MEMORIES

PASSPORT STAMPS

Mount Rainier
National Park

WA

EST. 1899 — 236,382 ACRES — 46° 51' 0" N, 121° 45' 0" W

DATE(S) I VISITED:

WHO I WENT WITH:

Sticker

SIGHTS & WILDLIFE

MY FAVORITE MEMORIES

PASSPORT STAMPS

Nez Perce
National Historical Park

ID, MT, OR, & WA

EST. 1965 — 4,564.93 ACRES — 46° 26' 49.2" N, 116° 49' 22.8" W

Sticker

DATE(S) I VISITED:

WHO I WENT WITH:

SIGHTS & WILDLIFE

MY FAVORITE MEMORIES

PASSPORT STAMPS

Noatak
National Preserve

AK

EST. 1978 — 6,587,071.39 ACRES — 68° 0' 0" N, 159° 30' 0" W

DATE(S) I VISITED:

Sticker

WHO I WENT WITH:

SIGHTS & WILDLIFE

MY FAVORITE MEMORIES

PASSPORT STAMPS

North Cascades
National Park

EST. 2020 — 72,346 ACRES — 38° 4' 12" N, 81° 4' 48" W

WA

Sticker

DATE(S) I VISITED:

WHO I WENT WITH:

SIGHTS & WILDLIFE

MY FAVORITE MEMORIES

PASSPORT STAMPS

Olympic
National Park

EST. 1968 — 504,781 ACRES — 48° 42' 0" N, 121° 12' 0" W

WA

DATE(S) I VISITED:

WHO I WENT WITH:

Sticker

SIGHTS & WILDLIFE

MY FAVORITE MEMORIES

PASSPORT STAMPS

453

Oregon Caves
National Monument and Preserve

EST. 1909 — 4,554.03 ACRES — 42° 5' 44" N, 123° 24' 21" W

OR

DATE(S) I VISITED:

Sticker

WHO I WENT WITH:

SIGHTS & WILDLIFE

MY FAVORITE MEMORIES

PASSPORT STAMPS

Ross Lake
National Recreation Area

EST. 1968 — 117,574.59 ACRES — 48° 40' 23" N, 121° 14' 43" W

WA

DATE(S) I VISITED:

Sticker

WHO I WENT WITH:

SIGHTS & WILDLIFE

MY FAVORITE MEMORIES

PASSPORT STAMPS

San Juan Island
National Historical Park

EST. 1966 — 2,145.56 ACRES — 48° 27' 21" N, 122° 59' 8" W

DATE(S) I VISITED:

WHO I WENT WITH:

Sticker

SIGHTS & WILDLIFE

MY FAVORITE MEMORIES

PASSPORT STAMPS

Sitka
National Historical Park

EST. 1972 — 116.29 ACRES — 57° 2' 55.97" N, 135° 18' 57.46" W

DATE(S) I VISITED:

WHO I WENT WITH:

Sticker

SIGHTS & WILDLIFE

MY FAVORITE MEMORIES

PASSPORT STAMPS

457

Whitman Mission
National Historic Site

EST. 1936 — 138.53 ACRES — 46° 2' 24" N, 118° 27' 41" W

DATE(S) I VISITED:

WHO I WENT WITH:

Sticker

SIGHTS & WILDLIFE

MY FAVORITE MEMORIES

PASSPORT STAMPS

Wrangell-St. Elias

AK

National Park and Preserve

EST. 1903 — 33,971 ACRES — 43° 34' 12" N, 103° 28' 48" W

DATE(S) I VISITED:

Sticker

WHO I WENT WITH:

SIGHTS & WILDLIFE

MY FAVORITE MEMORIES

PASSPORT STAMPS

Yukon-Charley Rivers
National Preserve

EST. 1978 — 2,526,512.44 ACRES — 65° 0' 0" N, 143° 30' 0" W

DATE(S) I VISITED:

Sticker

WHO I WENT WITH:

SIGHTS & WILDLIFE

MY FAVORITE MEMORIES

PASSPORT STAMPS

EST. _____ — _____ ACRES — ___° ___' ___" N, ___° ___' ___" W

DATE(S) I VISITED:

Sticker

WHO I WENT WITH:

SIGHTS & WILDLIFE

MY FAVORITE MEMORIES

PASSPORT STAMPS

_____

EST. _____ — _____ ACRES — ___° ___' ___" N, ___° ___' ___" W

DATE(S) I VISITED:

WHO I WENT WITH:

Sticker

SIGHTS & WILDLIFE

MY FAVORITE MEMORIES

PASSPORT STAMPS

_____

_____

— EST. _____ — _____ ACRES — __° __' __" N, __° __' __" W

DATE(S) I VISITED:

Sticker

WHO I WENT WITH:

SIGHTS & WILDLIFE

MY FAVORITE MEMORIES

PASSPORT STAMPS

_____

_____

EST. _____ — _____ ACRES — ___° ___' ___" N, ___° ___' ___" W

DATE(S) I VISITED:

Sticker

WHO I WENT WITH:

SIGHTS & WILDLIFE

MY FAVORITE MEMORIES

PASSPORT STAMPS

Index

Index

Index

Index

Made in the USA
Las Vegas, NV
13 February 2023

67481111R00258